Es

_____

Date

_____

THE
BIBLE
PROMISE
BOOK®

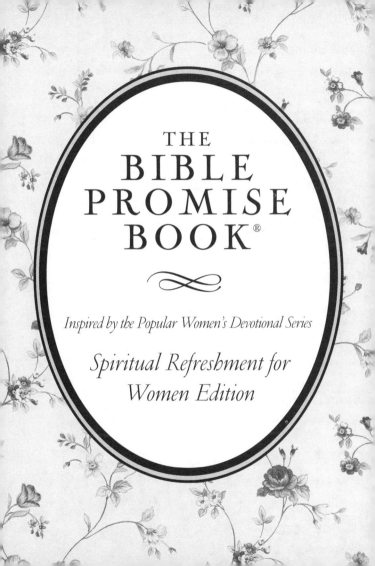

Inspired by the Popular Women's Devotional Series

Spiritual Refreshment for Women Edition

© 2014 by Barbour Publishing

Compiled by MariLee Parrish.

Print ISBN 978-1-62416-706-5
eBook Editions:
Adobe Digital Edition (.epub) 978-1-62836-331-9
Kindle and MobiPocket Edition (.prc) 978-1-62836-332-6

Published by Barbour Publishing, Inc., P.O. Box 719, Uhrichsville, Ohio 44683, www.barbourbooks.com

Our mission is to publish and distribute inspirational products offering exceptional value and biblical encouragement to the masses.

Member of the
Evangelical Christian
Publishers Association

Printed in the United States of America.

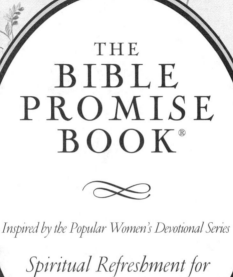

THE
BIBLE
PROMISE
BOOK®

Inspired by the Popular Women's Devotional Series

*Spiritual Refreshment for
Women Edition*

BARBOUR
PUBLISHING

Contents

Introduction

God's Word is full of promises.
And you know when He makes a promise,
you can trust it—*always*!

These inspiring Bible promises will refresh your spirit!
Each topic in this promise book was selected from our
popular Spiritual Refreshment for Women series—made up
of 14 faith-strengthening volumes—each featuring brief but
powerful devotional readings written specifically to speak to a
woman's everyday needs.

Allow each scripture selection to speak directly to your
heart as you draw ever closer to your heavenly Father.

The Publishers

Everyday Blessings

Blessings are God's gifts to us—simple or great, they are produced by the overflow of His great love. We recognize them most often when they include a reprieve from sickness or a financial provision for a critical need. But we are prone to take for granted the sunshine that lights our days and lifts our spirits, the affection of friends and family, the kindness of strangers. . .

These Bible promises will open your eyes to the blessings all around you and encourage you to bask in the loving-kindness of our awesome God. As you read through these scriptures, you will see God's hand in every aspect of your life, filling it with goodness, hope, joy, and peace.

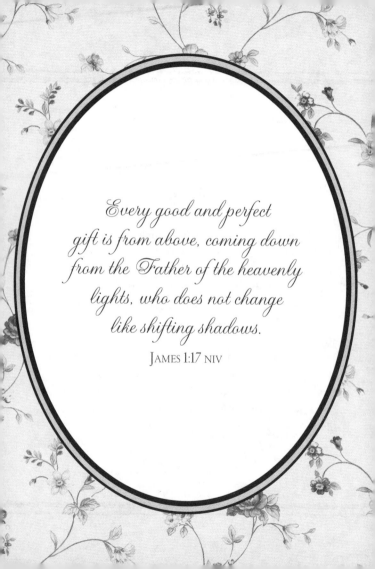

Every good and perfect
gift is from above, coming down
from the Father of the heavenly
lights, who does not change
like shifting shadows.

JAMES 1:17 NIV

"All who are victorious will inherit all these blessings,
and I will be their God, and they will be my children."
REVELATION 21:7 NLT

Through Christ Jesus, God has blessed the Gentiles
with the same blessing he promised to Abraham,
so that we who are believers might receive the
promised Holy Spirit through faith.
GALATIANS 3:14 NLT

But the wisdom that comes from God is first of all pure,
then peaceful, gentle, and easy to please. This wisdom is
always ready to help those who are troubled and to
do good for others. It is always fair and honest.
JAMES 3:17 NCV

But let all who take refuge in you be glad; let them
ever sing for joy. Spread your protection over them,
that those who love your name may rejoice in you.
Surely, LORD, you bless the righteous; you surround
them with your favor as with a shield.
PSALM 5:11–12 NIV

Finally, all of you, have unity of spirit, sympathy, love for one another, a tender heart, and a humble mind. Do not repay evil for evil or abuse for abuse; but, on the contrary, repay with a blessing. It is for this that you were called—that you might inherit a blessing. For "Those who desire life and desire to see good days, let them keep their tongues from evil and their lips from speaking deceit; let them turn away from evil and do good; let them seek peace and pursue it. For the eyes of the Lord are on the righteous, and his ears are open to their prayer. But the face of the Lord is against those who do evil."

1 PETER 3:8–12 NRSV

"Bring all the tithes into the storehouse so there will be enough food in my Temple. If you do," says the LORD of Heaven's Armies, "I will open the windows of heaven for you. I will pour out a blessing so great you won't have enough room to take it in! Try it! Put me to the test!"

MALACHI 3:10 NLT

He said also to the one who had invited him,
"When you give a luncheon or a dinner, do not invite
your friends or your brothers or your relatives or rich
neighbors, in case they may invite you in return, and you
would be repaid. But when you give a banquet, invite the poor,
the crippled, the lame, and the blind. And you will be blessed,
because they cannot repay you, for you will be repaid
at the resurrection of the righteous."
LUKE 14:12–14 NRSV

This service that you perform is not only supplying
the needs of the Lord's people but is also overflowing
in many expressions of thanks to God.
2 CORINTHIANS 9:12 NIV

The LORD gives strength to his people;
the LORD blesses his people with peace.
PSALM 29:11 NIV

Remember your promise to me;
it is my only hope. Your promise revives me;
it comforts me in all my troubles.
PSALM 119:49–50 NLT

Those who live only to satisfy their own sinful
nature will harvest decay and death from that sinful nature.
But those who live to please the Spirit will harvest
everlasting life from the Spirit. So let's not get tired of doing
what is good. At just the right time we will reap a harvest
of blessing if we don't give up. Therefore, whenever we
have the opportunity, we should do good to everyone—
especially to those in the family of faith.
GALATIANS 6:8–10 NLT

I remain confident of this: I will see the goodness of
the LORD in the land of the living. Wait for the LORD;
be strong and take heart and wait for the LORD.
PSALM 27:13–14 NIV

The LORD is the strength of his people, a fortress of
salvation for his anointed one. Save your people and bless your
inheritance; be their shepherd and carry them forever.
PSALM 28:8–9 NIV

Though I am surrounded by troubles, you will protect me
from the anger of my enemies. You reach out your hand, and
the power of your right hand saves me. The Lord will work
out his plans for my life—for your faithful love, O Lord,
endures forever. Don't abandon me, for you made me.
PSALM 138:7–8 NLT

"The God who made the world and everything in it is the
Lord of heaven and earth and does not live in temples built
by human hands. And he is not served by human hands,
as if he needed anything. Rather, he himself gives
everyone life and breath and everything else."
ACTS 17:24–25 NIV

He has made everything beautiful in its time.
He has also set eternity in the human heart; yet no one
can fathom what God has done from beginning to end.
ECCLESIASTES 3:11 NIV

All praise to God, the Father of our Lord Jesus Christ, who has blessed us with every spiritual blessing in the heavenly realms because we are united with Christ.

EPHESIANS 1:3 NLT

"From one man he made all the nations, that they should inhabit the whole earth; and he marked out their appointed times in history and the boundaries of their lands. God did this so that they would seek him and perhaps reach out for him and find him, though he is not far from any one of us."

ACTS 17:26–27 NIV

LORD, you alone are my inheritance, my cup of blessing. You guard all that is mine. The land you have given me is a pleasant land. What a wonderful inheritance!

PSALM 16:5–6 NLT

LORD, you are mine! I promise to obey your words! With all my heart I want your blessings. Be merciful as you promised. I pondered the direction of my life, and I turned to follow your laws.

PSALM 119:57–59 NLT

Blessed is the one who does not walk in step with
the wicked or stand in the way that sinners take or sit
in the company of mockers, but whose delight is in the law
of the LORD, and who meditates on his law day and night.
That person is like a tree planted by streams of water,
which yields its fruit in season and whose leaf
does not wither—whatever they do prospers.
PSALM 1:1–3 NIV

You prepare a feast for me in the presence of my enemies.
You honor me by anointing my head with oil. My cup
overflows with blessings. Surely your goodness and
unfailing love will pursue me all the days of my life,
and I will live in the house of the LORD forever.
PSALM 23:5–6 NLT

"And if I go and prepare a place for you,
I will come back and take you to be with
me that you also may be where I am."
JOHN 14:3 NIV

"Today I have given you the choice between life and death, between blessings and curses. Now I call on heaven and earth to witness the choice you make. Oh, that you would choose life, so that you and your descendants might live! You can make this choice by loving the LORD your God, obeying him, and committing yourself firmly to him. This is the key to your life. And if you love and obey the LORD, you will live long in the land the LORD swore to give your ancestors Abraham, Isaac, and Jacob."

DEUTERONOMY 30:19–20 NLT

"Give, and it will be given to you. A good measure, pressed down, shaken together and running over, will be poured into your lap. For with the measure you use, it will be measured to you."

LUKE 6:38 NIV

Therefore, since we receive a kingdom which cannot be shaken, let us show gratitude, by which we may offer to God an acceptable service with reverence and awe.

HEBREWS 12:28 NASB

God be gracious to us and bless us, and cause His
face to shine upon us—Selah. That Your way may be known
on the earth, Your salvation among all nations. Let the peoples
praise You, O God; let all the peoples praise You.

PSALM 67:1–3 NASB

Blessings are on the head of the righteous, but the mouth of
the wicked conceals violence. The memory of the righteous is
blessed, but the name of the wicked will rot. The wise of heart
will receive commands, but a babbling fool will be ruined.
He who walks in integrity walks securely.

PROVERBS 10:6–9 NASB

Therefore repent and return, so that your sins
may be wiped away, in order that times of refreshing
may come from the presence of the Lord.

ACTS 3:19 NASB

I give you thanks, O LORD, with all my heart; I will
sing your praises before the gods. I bow before your holy
Temple as I worship. I praise your name for your
unfailing love and faithfulness; for your promises
are backed by all the honor of your name.

PSALM 138:1–2 NLT

How great is the goodness you have stored up for
those who fear you. You lavish it on those who come
to you for protection, blessing them before the watching
world. You hide them in the shelter of your presence,
safe from those who conspire against them. You shelter
them in your presence, far from accusing tongues.

PSALM 31:19–20 NLT

Blessed be the God and Father of our Lord Jesus Christ,
who has blessed us with every spiritual blessing in the
heavenly places in Christ, just as He chose us in Him before
the foundation of the world, that we would be holy and
blameless before Him. In love He predestined us to adoption
as sons through Jesus Christ to Himself, according to the kind
intention of His will, to the praise of the glory of His grace,
which He freely bestowed on us in the Beloved.

EPHESIANS 1:3–6 NASB

Everyday Comfort

One day we will reside in heaven where love, joy, and peace prevail. But until then, God has promised us His comfort. No matter what we face in this lifetime, no matter what calamity comes our way—big or small— God has vowed never to let go of our hands.

The following scriptures are gentle reminders that you are never alone in your troubles. If you trust God, He will be there in good times and bad, pouring out His love, providing wisdom and guidance, listening to your hurting heart, shouldering your burdens, and bringing you safely through to the other side.

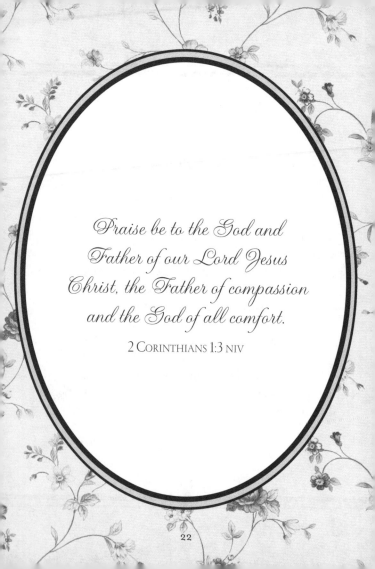

Praise be to the God and
Father of our Lord Jesus
Christ, the Father of compassion
and the God of all comfort.

2 CORINTHIANS 1:3 NIV

At that time Jesus said, "I praise you, Father,
Lord of heaven and earth, because you have hidden these
things from the wise and learned, and revealed them to little
children. Yes, Father, for this is what you were pleased to do. . . .
"Come to me, all you who are weary and burdened,
and I will give you rest. Take my yoke upon you and
learn from me, for I am gentle and humble in heart,
and you will find rest for your souls.
For my yoke is easy and my burden is light."
MATTHEW 11:25–26, 28–30 NIV

LORD, you know the hopes of the helpless.
Surely you will hear their cries and comfort them.
PSALM 10:17 NLT

Yea, though I walk through the valley of the
shadow of death, I will fear no evil: for thou
art with me; thy rod and thy staff they comfort me.
PSALM 23:4 KJV

Answer my prayers, O LORD, for your unfailing
love is wonderful. Take care of me, for your mercy
is so plentiful. Don't hide from your servant; answer
me quickly, for I am in deep trouble! Come and
redeem me; free me from my enemies.

PSALM 69:16–18 NLT

Shout for joy, you heavens; rejoice, you earth;
burst into song, you mountains! For the
LORD comforts his people and will have
compassion on his afflicted ones.

ISAIAH 49:13 NIV

The Sovereign LORD has given me his words of wisdom,
so that I know how to comfort the weary. Morning by
morning he wakens me and opens my understanding to
his will. The Sovereign LORD has spoken to me, and I
have listened. I have not rebelled or turned away.

ISAIAH 50:4–5 NLT

Remember your promise to me, your servant;
it gives me hope. When I suffer, this comforts me:
Your promise gives me life.

PSALM 119:49–50 NCV

"I, yes I, am the one who comforts you. So why are you afraid
of mere humans, who wither like the grass and disappear?
Yet you have forgotten the LORD, your Creator, the one who
stretched out the sky like a canopy and laid the foundations
of the earth. Will you remain in constant dread of human
oppressors? Will you continue to fear the anger of your
enemies? Where is their fury and anger now? It is gone!"

ISAIAH 51:12–13 NLT

I know, O LORD, that your judgments are right,
and that in faithfulness you have humbled me.
Let your steadfast love become my comfort according
to your promise to your servant. Let your mercy come
to me, that I may live; for your law is my delight.

PSALM 119:75–77 NRSV

But Lord, you are a God who shows mercy and is
kind. You don't become angry quickly. You have great
love and faithfulness. Turn to me and have mercy.
Give me, your servant, strength. Save me, the son of
your female servant. Show me a sign of your goodness.
When my enemies look, they will be ashamed.
You, LORD, have helped me and comforted me.
PSALM 86:15–17 NCV

Though you have made me see troubles,
many and bitter, you will restore my life again;
from the depths of the earth you will again bring me up.
You will increase my honor and comfort me once more.
PSALM 71:20–21 NIV

Blessed are the poor in spirit: for theirs is the
kingdom of heaven. Blessed are they that mourn:
for they shall be comforted. Blessed are the meek:
for they shall inherit the earth.
MATTHEW 5:3–5 KJV

The LORD wants to show his mercy to you. He wants
to rise and comfort you. The LORD is a fair God, and
everyone who waits for his help will be happy. You people
who live on Mount Zion in Jerusalem will not cry anymore.
The LORD will hear your crying, and he will comfort you.
When he hears you, he will help you.

ISAIAH 30:18–19 NCV

Jesus said, "Don't let your hearts be troubled. Trust in
God, and trust in me. There are many rooms in my
Father's house; I would not tell you this if it were not true.
I am going there to prepare a place for you. After I go and
prepare a place for you, I will come back and take you
to be with me so that you may be where I am. You know
the way to the place where I am going."

JOHN 14:1–4 NCV

"I will ask the Father, and he will give you another Helper to be with you forever—the Spirit of truth. The world cannot accept him, because it does not see him or know him. But you know him, because he lives with you and he will be in you."
JOHN 14:16–17 NCV

The LORD is a shelter for the oppressed, a refuge in times of trouble. Those who know your name trust in you, for you, O LORD, do not abandon those who search for you.
PSALM 9:9–10 NLT

The one thing I ask of the LORD—the thing I seek most—is to live in the house of the LORD all the days of my life, delighting in the LORD's perfections and meditating in his Temple. For he will conceal me there when troubles come; he will hide me in his sanctuary. He will place me out of reach on a high rock.
PSALM 27:4–5 NLT

Humble yourselves therefore under the mighty hand of God, that he may exalt you in due time: Casting all your care upon him; for he careth for you.
1 PETER 5:6–7 KJV

You keep track of all my sorrows. You have collected
all my tears in your bottle. You have recorded each one
in your book. My enemies will retreat when I call to you
for help. This I know: God is on my side! I praise God for
what he has promised; yes, I praise the LORD for what he has
promised. I trust in God, so why should I be afraid?
What can mere mortals do to me?

PSALM 56:8–11 NLT

I love the LORD, for he heard my voice; he heard
my cry for mercy. Because he turned his ear to me,
I will call on him as long as I live.

PSALM 116:1–2 NIV

The LORD is gracious and righteous; our God is
full of compassion. The LORD protects the unwary;
when I was brought low, he saved me.

PSALM 116:5–6 NIV

The LORD is good, a refuge in times of trouble.
He cares for those who trust in him.

NAHUM 1:7 NIV

There is a time for everything, and a season for every
activity under the heavens: a time to be born and a time
to die, a time to plant and a time to uproot, a time to kill
and a time to heal, a time to tear down and a time to build,
a time to weep and a time to laugh, a time to mourn and a
time to dance, a time to scatter stones and a time to gather
them, a time to embrace and a time to refrain from embracing,
a time to search and a time to give up, a time to keep and
a time to throw away, a time to tear and a time to mend,
a time to be silent and a time to speak, a time to love and a
time to hate, a time for war and a time for peace.
ECCLESIASTES 3:1–8 NIV

It is of the LORD's mercies that we are not consumed,
because his compassions fail not. They are new
every morning: great is thy faithfulness.
LAMENTATIONS 3:22–23 KJV

Then you will walk on your way securely and your
foot will not stumble. If you sit down, you will not be afraid;
when you lie down, your sleep will be sweet. Do not be afraid
of sudden panic, or of the storm that strikes the wicked;
for the LORD will be your confidence and will keep
your foot from being caught.
PROVERBS 3:23–26 NRSV

"But when the Father sends the Advocate as my
representative—that is, the Holy Spirit—he will teach you
everything and will remind you of everything I have told
you. I am leaving you with a gift—peace of mind and heart.
And the peace I give is a gift the world cannot give.
So don't be troubled or afraid."
JOHN 14:26–27 NLT

You will say in that day: I will give thanks to you, O LORD,
for though you were angry with me, your anger turned away,
and you comforted me. Surely God is my salvation; I will
trust, and will not be afraid, for the LORD GOD is my strength
and my might; he has become my salvation.
ISAIAH 12:1–2 NRSV

I say to myself, "The LORD is my inheritance; therefore, I will hope in him!" The LORD is good to those who depend on him, to those who search for him. So it is good to wait quietly for salvation from the LORD.

LAMENTATIONS 3:24–26 NLT

Then Jesus said to his disciples: "Therefore I tell you, do not worry about your life, what you will eat; or about your body, what you will wear. For life is more than food, and the body more than clothes. Consider the ravens: They do not sow or reap, they have no storeroom or barn; yet God feeds them. And how much more valuable you are than birds! Who of you by worrying can add a single hour to your life? Since you cannot do this very little thing, why do you worry about the rest?"

LUKE 12:22–26 NIV

Everyday Encouragement

Some days we need a gentle hand to pick us up and a voice to whisper encouragement in our ears. Life can be challenging, and when trials come our way, we may feel discouraged and defeated. But God does not fail us, no matter what our days hold.

Each of the following Bible promises will comfort you through all your troubles. Read on, and feel the touch of the heavenly Father's tender hand and find strength for today and every day.

May our Lord Jesus
Christ himself and God our
Father. . .encourage your
hearts and strengthen you.

2 Thessalonians 2:16–17 niv

No temptation has overtaken you that is not common to man. God is faithful, and he will not let you be tempted beyond your ability, but with the temptation he will also provide the way of escape, that you may be able to endure it.
1 Corinthians 10:13 esv

Brothers and sisters, we taught you how to live in a way that will please God, and you are living that way. Now we ask and encourage you in the Lord Jesus to live that way even more.
1 Thessalonians 4:1 ncv

Do all things without grumbling or disputing, that you may be blameless and innocent, children of God without blemish in the midst of a crooked and twisted generation, among whom you shine as lights in the world, holding fast to the word of life.
Philippians 2:14–16 esv

Jesus said to the people who believed in him, "You are truly my disciples if you remain faithful to my teachings. And you will know the truth, and the truth will set you free."
John 8:31–32 nlt

We encouraged you, we urged you, and we insisted
that you live good lives for God, who calls you to his glorious
kingdom. Also, we always thank God because when you
heard his message from us, you accepted it as the word
of God, not the words of humans. And it really is God's
message which works in you who believe.

1 Thessalonians 2:12–13 ncv

For you created my inmost being; you knit me together
in my mother's womb. I praise you because I am fearfully
and wonderfully made; your works are wonderful, I know
that full well. My frame was not hidden from you when I
was made in the secret place, when I was woven together in
the depths of the earth. Your eyes saw my unformed body;
all the days ordained for me were written in your
book before one of them came to be.

Psalm 139:13–16 niv

We have confidence in the Lord that you are
doing and will continue to do the things we
command. May the Lord direct your hearts
into God's love and Christ's perseverance.

2 Thessalonians 3:4–5 niv

Jesus died for us so that we can live together with him,
whether we are alive or dead when he comes. So
encourage each other and give each other strength,
just as you are doing now. Now, brothers and sisters,
we ask you to appreciate those who work hard among you,
who lead you in the Lord and teach you.

1 Thessalonians 5:10–12 NCV

The humble will see their God at work and be glad.
Let all who seek God's help be encouraged.

Psalm 69:32 NLT

Help me understand the meaning of your commandments,
and I will meditate on your wonderful deeds.
I weep with sorrow; encourage me by your word.

Psalm 119:27–28 NLT

As soon as I pray, you answer me;
you encourage me by giving me strength.

Psalm 138:3 NLT

Therefore if there is any encouragement in Christ, if there is any consolation of love, if there is any fellowship of the Spirit, if any affection and compassion, make my joy complete by being of the same mind, maintaining the same love, united in spirit, intent on one purpose. Do nothing from selfishness or empty conceit, but with humility of mind regard one another as more important than yourselves; do not merely look out for your own personal interests, but also for the interests of others.

PHILIPPIANS 2:1–4 NASB

I want them to be encouraged and knit together by strong ties of love. I want them to have complete confidence that they understand God's mysterious plan, which is Christ himself. In him lie hidden all the treasures of wisdom and knowledge.

COLOSSIANS 2:2–3 NLT

Then, by the will of God, I will be able to come to you with a joyful heart, and we will be an encouragement to each other. And now may God, who gives us his peace, be with you all. Amen.

ROMANS 15:32–33 NLT

"Don't be afraid," he said, "for you are very precious to God. Peace! Be encouraged! Be strong!" As he spoke these words to me, I suddenly felt stronger and said to him, "Please speak to me, my lord, for you have strengthened me."
DANIEL 10:19 NLT

In his grace, God has given us different gifts for doing certain things well. So if God has given you the ability to prophesy, speak out with as much faith as God has given you. If your gift is serving others, serve them well. If you are a teacher, teach well. If your gift is to encourage others, be encouraging. If it is giving, give generously. If God has given you leadership ability, take the responsibility seriously. And if you have a gift for showing kindness to others, do it gladly.
ROMANS 12:6–8 NLT

Finally, brothers and sisters, rejoice! Strive for full restoration, encourage one another, be of one mind, live in peace. And the God of love and peace will be with you.
2 CORINTHIANS 13:11 NIV

Let everything you say be good and helpful, so that your
words will be an encouragement to those who hear them.
And do not bring sorrow to God's Holy Spirit by the way
you live. Remember, he has identified you as his own,
guaranteeing that you will be saved on the day of redemption.
EPHESIANS 4:29–30 NLT

You hem me in behind and before, and you lay
your hand upon me. Such knowledge is too
wonderful for me, too lofty for me to attain.
PSALM 139:5–6 NIV

Many are the plans in a person's heart,
but it is the LORD's purpose that prevails.
PROVERBS 19:21 NIV

Work willingly at whatever you do, as though you were
working for the Lord rather than for people. Remember
that the Lord will give you an inheritance as your reward,
and that the Master you are serving is Christ.
COLOSSIANS 3:23–24 NLT

So we have been greatly encouraged in the midst of our troubles and suffering, dear brothers and sisters, because you have remained strong in your faith. It gives us new life to know that you are standing firm in the Lord.

1 Thessalonians 3:7–8 nlt

You will always harvest what you plant. Those who live only to satisfy their own sinful nature will harvest decay and death from that sinful nature. But those who live to please the Spirit will harvest everlasting life from the Spirit.

Galatians 6:7–8 nlt

"Ask, and it will be given to you; seek, and you will find; knock, and it will be opened to you. For everyone who asks receives, and the one who seeks finds, and to the one who knocks it will be opened."

Matthew 7:7–8 esv

May God, who gives this patience and encouragement, help you live in complete harmony with each other, as is fitting for followers of Christ Jesus. Then all of you can join together with one voice, giving praise and glory to God, the Father of our Lord Jesus Christ. Therefore, accept each other just as Christ has accepted you so that God will be given glory.

ROMANS 15:5–7 NLT

The LORD is compassionate and gracious, slow to anger, abounding in love. He will not always accuse, nor will he harbor his anger forever; he does not treat us as our sins deserve or repay us according to our iniquities. For as high as the heavens are above the earth, so great is his love for those who fear him; as far as the east is from the west, so far has he removed our transgressions from us. As a father has compassion on his children, so the LORD has compassion on those who fear him.

PSALM 103:8–13 NIV

Even the wilderness and desert will be glad in those days.
The wasteland will rejoice and blossom with spring crocuses.
Yes, there will be an abundance of flowers and singing and
joy! The deserts will become as green as the mountains of
Lebanon, as lovely as Mount Carmel or the plain of Sharon.
There the LORD will display his glory, the splendor of our
God. With this news, strengthen those who have tired hands,
and encourage those who have weak knees. Say to those with
fearful hearts, "Be strong, and do not fear, for your God is
coming to destroy your enemies. He is coming to save you."
ISAIAH 35:1–4 NLT

May our Lord Jesus Christ himself and God our Father
encourage you and strengthen you in every good thing you
do and say. God loved us, and through his grace he gave us
a good hope and encouragement that continues forever.
2 THESSALONIANS 2:16–17 NCV

We who are strong must be considerate of those who
are sensitive about things like this. We must not just
please ourselves. We should help others do what is right
and build them up in the Lord. For even Christ didn't live
to please himself. As the Scriptures say, "The insults of those
who insult you, O God, have fallen on me." Such things
were written in the Scriptures long ago to teach us. And
the Scriptures give us hope and encouragement as we wait
patiently for God's promises to be fulfilled.
ROMANS 15:1–4 NLT

I pray that your partnership with us in the faith may
be effective in deepening your understanding of every good
thing we share for the sake of Christ. Your love has given
me great joy and encouragement, because you, brother,
have refreshed the hearts of the Lord's people.
PHILEMON 1:6–7 NIV

See to it, brothers and sisters, that none of you has a sinful,
unbelieving heart that turns away from the living God. But
encourage one another daily, as long as it is called "Today," so
that none of you may be hardened by sin's deceitfulness.
HEBREWS 3:12–13 NIV

Everyday Faith

God places utmost importance on faith, and the reason is simple: faith is the key by which we gain access to Him. How can we love Him if we aren't sure He exists? How can we trust Him if we aren't sure He wants to be part of our lives? By faith we come into the heavenly Father's presence and establish a relationship with Him.

Each of the following Bible promises will open your eyes to faith and help you take faith from word to concept to actual experience. As you read through these scripture selections, you will hear God's voice calling you to place your faith in Him in every area of your life.

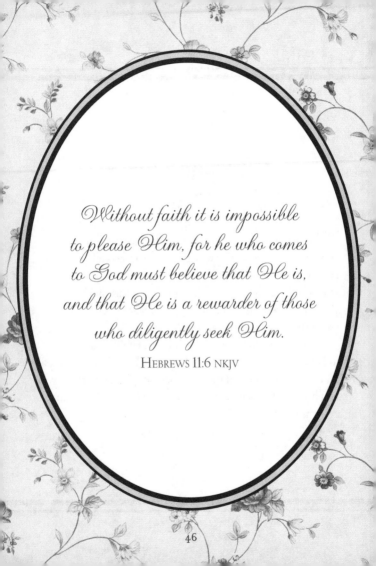

Without faith it is impossible to please Him, for he who comes to God must believe that He is, and that He is a rewarder of those who diligently seek Him.

HEBREWS 11:6 NKJV

But Jesus spoke to them at once. "Don't be afraid,"
he said. "Take courage. I am here!"
Then Peter called to him, "Lord, if it's really you,
tell me to come to you, walking on the water."
"Yes, come," Jesus said.
So Peter went over the side of the boat and walked
on the water toward Jesus. But when he saw the
strong wind and the waves, he was terrified and
began to sink. "Save me, Lord!" he shouted.
Jesus immediately reached out and grabbed him.
"You have so little faith," Jesus said. "Why did you doubt me?"
When they climbed back into the boat, the wind stopped.
Then the disciples worshiped him. "You really are the
Son of God!" they exclaimed.
MATTHEW 14:27–33 NLT

God, who knows the heart, showed that he accepted
them by giving the Holy Spirit to them, just as he
did to us. He did not discriminate between us
and them, for he purified their hearts by faith.
ACTS 15:8–9 NIV

"Have faith in God," Jesus answered. "Truly I tell you, if anyone says to this mountain, 'Go, throw yourself into the sea,' and does not doubt in their heart but believes that what they say will happen, it will be done for them. Therefore I tell you, whatever you ask for in prayer, believe that you have received it, and it will be yours. And when you stand praying, if you hold anything against anyone, forgive them, so that your Father in heaven may forgive you your sins."

MARK 11:22–25 NIV

The apostles said to the Lord,
"Show us how to increase our faith."
The Lord answered, "If you had faith even as small as a mustard seed, you could say to this mulberry tree, 'May you be uprooted and thrown into the sea,' and it would obey you!"

LUKE 17:5–6 NLT

Surely, Lord, you bless the righteous; you surround them with your favor as with a shield.

PSALM 5:12 NIV

"God clothes the grass in the field, which is alive today but tomorrow is thrown into the fire. So you can be even more sure that God will clothe you. Don't have so little faith!"
MATTHEW 6:30 NCV

For I am not ashamed of this Good News about Christ. It is the power of God at work, saving everyone who believes—the Jew first and also the Gentile. This Good News tells us how God makes us right in his sight. This is accomplished from start to finish by faith. As the Scriptures say, "It is through faith that a righteous person has life."
ROMANS 1:16–17 NLT

When people work, their wages are not a gift, but something they have earned. But people are counted as righteous, not because of their work, but because of their faith in God who forgives sinners.
ROMANS 4:4–5 NLT

Suddenly a furious storm came up on the lake,
so that the waves swept over the boat. But Jesus
was sleeping. The disciples went and woke him,
saying, "Lord, save us! We're going to drown!"
He replied, "You of little faith, why are you so afraid?"
Then he got up and rebuked the winds and the waves,
and it was completely calm. The men were amazed
and asked, "What kind of man is this?
Even the winds and the waves obey him!"
MATTHEW 8:24–27 NIV

"All those who stand before others and say they believe
in me, I will say before my Father in heaven that they
belong to me. But all who stand before others and say
they do not believe in me, I will say before my Father
in heaven that they do not belong to me."
MATTHEW 10:32–33 NCV

"He who is faithful in a very little thing is faithful
also in much; and he who is unrighteous in a very
little thing is unrighteous also in much."
LUKE 16:10 NASB

As Jesus approached Jericho, a blind beggar was sitting beside
the road. When he heard the noise of a crowd going past,
he asked what was happening. They told him that Jesus the
Nazarene was going by. So he began shouting,
"Jesus, Son of David, have mercy on me!"
"Be quiet!" the people in front yelled at him.
But he only shouted louder, "Son of David, have mercy on me!"
When Jesus heard him, he stopped and ordered that the man
be brought to him. As the man came near, Jesus asked him,
"What do you want me to do for you?"
"Lord," he said, "I want to see!"
And Jesus said, "All right, receive your sight! Your faith has
healed you." Instantly the man could see, and he followed
Jesus, praising God. And all who saw it praised God, too.
LUKE 18:35–43 NLT

We who are strong in faith should help the weak
with their weaknesses, and not please only ourselves.
Let each of us please our neighbors for their good,
to help them be stronger in faith.
ROMANS 15:1–2 NCV

But now God has shown us a way to be made right with him without keeping the requirements of the law, as was promised in the writings of Moses and the prophets long ago. We are made right with God by placing our faith in Jesus Christ. And this is true for everyone who believes, no matter who we are. For everyone has sinned; we all fall short of God's glorious standard.

ROMANS 3:21–23 NLT

Never be lacking in zeal, but keep your spiritual fervor, serving the Lord. Be joyful in hope, patient in affliction, faithful in prayer. Share with the Lord's people who are in need. Practice hospitality.

ROMANS 12:11–13 NIV

I may have the gift of prophecy. I may understand all the secret things of God and have all knowledge, and I may have faith so great I can move mountains. But even with all these things, if I do not have love, then I am nothing.

1 CORINTHIANS 13:2 NCV

And all are justified freely by his grace through the redemption that came by Christ Jesus. God presented Christ as a sacrifice of atonement, through the shedding of his blood—to be received by faith. He did this to demonstrate his righteousness, because in his forbearance he had left the sins committed beforehand unpunished—he did it to demonstrate his righteousness at the present time, so as to be just and the one who justifies those who have faith in Jesus.

ROMANS 3:24–26 NIV

If you declare with your mouth, "Jesus is Lord," and believe in your heart that God raised him from the dead, you will be saved. For it is with your heart that you believe and are justified, and it is with your mouth that you profess your faith and are saved. As Scripture says, "Anyone who believes in him will never be put to shame."

ROMANS 10:9–11 NIV

So people receive God's promise by having faith. This happens
so the promise can be a free gift. Then all of Abraham's
children can have that promise. It is not only for those who
live under the law of Moses but for anyone who lives with
faith like that of Abraham, who is the father of us all.

ROMANS 4:16 NCV

Since we have been made right with God by our faith,
we have peace with God. This happened through our Lord
Jesus Christ, who through our faith has brought us into that
blessing of God's grace that we now enjoy. And we are happy
because of the hope we have of sharing God's glory.

ROMANS 5:1–2 NCV

Jesus replied: " 'Love the Lord your God with all
your heart and with all your soul and with all your
mind.' This is the first and greatest commandment.
And the second is like it: 'Love your neighbor as
yourself.' All the Law and the Prophets hang on
these two commandments."

MATTHEW 22:37–40 NIV

So do we have a reason to brag about ourselves? No! And why not? It is the way of faith that stops all bragging, not the way of trying to obey the law. A person is made right with God through faith, not through obeying the law. Is God only the God of the Jews? Is he not also the God of those who are not Jews? Of course he is, because there is only one God. He will make Jews right with him by their faith, and he will also make those who are not Jews right with him through their faith. So do we destroy the law by following the way of faith? No! Faith causes us to be what the law truly wants.

ROMANS 3:27–31 NCV

We have much sadness, but we are always rejoicing. We are poor, but we are making many people rich in faith. We have nothing, but really we have everything.

2 CORINTHIANS 6:10 NCV

All these things are for you. And so the grace of God
that is being given to more and more people will bring
increasing thanks to God for his glory. So we do not give
up. Our physical body is becoming older and weaker,
but our spirit inside us is made new every day. We have
small troubles for a while now, but they are helping us gain
an eternal glory that is much greater than the troubles.
2 CORINTHIANS 4:15–17 NCV

For it is by grace you have been saved, through faith—
and this is not from yourselves, it is the gift of God—
not by works, so that no one can boast.
EPHESIANS 2:8–9 NIV

In addition to all this, take up the shield of faith, with which
you can extinguish all the flaming arrows of the evil one.
EPHESIANS 6:16 NIV

Everyday Grace

Grace is a gift we did nothing to earn. It comes to us in many shapes and forms. It is a birdsong and the sun on our faces on a day when nothing else seems to go right; a child's hand in ours; a friend's understanding smile. And most of all, grace is the gift of God's unconditional love. Grace is Jesus, the One who saves us and heals us and never stops loving us.

These selected Bible promises will remind you of the many gifts of grace that fill our daily lives. God's grace is always there, waiting to be noticed, waiting to be enjoyed.

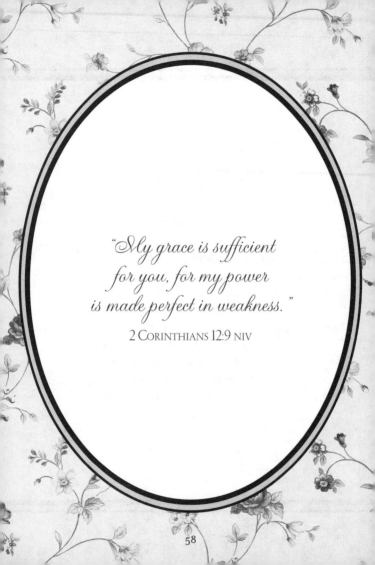

"My grace is sufficient
for you, for my power
is made perfect in weakness."

2 Corinthians 12:9 NIV

The Lord is my rock, my protection, my Savior.
My God is my rock. I can run to him for safety.
He is my shield and my saving strength, my defender.

PSALM 18:2 NCV

But God's mercy is great, and he loved us very much.
Though we were spiritually dead because of the things
we did against God, he gave us new life with Christ. You
have been saved by God's grace. And he raised us up
with Christ and gave us a seat with him in the heavens.
He did this for those in Christ Jesus.

EPHESIANS 2:4–6 NCV

And now the prize awaits me—the crown of
righteousness, which the Lord, the righteous Judge,
will give me on the day of his return. And the
prize is not just for me but for all who eagerly
look forward to his appearing.

2 TIMOTHY 4:8 NLT

One who loves a pure heart and who speaks with grace will have the king for a friend. The eyes of the LORD keep watch over knowledge, but he frustrates the words of the unfaithful.

PROVERBS 22:11–12 NIV

God's law was given so that all people could see how sinful they were. But as people sinned more and more, God's wonderful grace became more abundant. So just as sin ruled over all people and brought them to death, now God's wonderful grace rules instead, giving us right standing with God and resulting in eternal life through Jesus Christ our Lord.

ROMANS 5:20–21 NLT

May God our Father and the Lord Jesus Christ give you grace and peace. I always thank my God for you and for the gracious gifts he has given you, now that you belong to Christ Jesus.

1 CORINTHIANS 1:3–4 NLT

But there is a great difference between Adam's sin and God's gracious gift. For the sin of this one man, Adam, brought death to many. But even greater is God's wonderful grace and his gift of forgiveness to many through this other man, Jesus Christ. And the result of God's gracious gift is very different from the result of that one man's sin. For Adam's sin led to condemnation, but God's free gift leads to our being made right with God, even though we are guilty of many sins.

ROMANS 5:15–16 NLT

Everyone has sinned and fallen short of God's glorious standard, and all need to be made right with God by his grace, which is a free gift. They need to be made free from sin through Jesus Christ. God sent him to die in our place to take away our sins. We receive forgiveness through faith in the blood of Jesus' death. This showed that God always does what is right and fair, as in the past when he was patient and did not punish people for their sins.

ROMANS 3:23–25 NCV

But whatever I am now, it is all because God poured out
his special favor on me—and not without results. For I have
worked harder than any of the other apostles; yet it was not
I but God who was working through me by his grace.

1 CORINTHIANS 15:10 NLT

May God our Father and the Lord Jesus Christ give
you grace and peace. All praise to God, the Father
of our Lord Jesus Christ. God is our merciful
Father and the source of all comfort.

2 CORINTHIANS 1:2–3 NLT

We can say with confidence and a clear conscience that we
have lived with a God-given holiness and sincerity in all our
dealings. We have depended on God's grace, not on our own
human wisdom. That is how we have conducted ourselves
before the world, and especially toward you.

2 CORINTHIANS 1:12 NLT

Sin will not be your master, because you
are not under law but under God's grace.

ROMANS 6:14 NCV

For the LORD God is our sun and our shield. He gives us grace and glory. The LORD will withhold no good thing from those who do what is right. O LORD of Heaven's Armies, what joy for those who trust in you.

PSALM 84:11–12 NLT

"On that day the LORD will shield those who live in Jerusalem, so that the feeblest among them will be like David, and the house of David will be like God, like the angel of the LORD going before them. On that day I will set out to destroy all the nations that attack Jerusalem.

And I will pour out on the house of David and the inhabitants of Jerusalem a spirit of grace and supplication. They will look on me, the one they have pierced, and they will mourn for him as one mourns for an only child, and grieve bitterly for him as one grieves for a firstborn son."

ZECHARIAH 12:8–10 NIV

For you, O Lord, are good and forgiving, abounding in steadfast love to all who call upon you. Give ear, O LORD, to my prayer; listen to my plea for grace. In the day of my trouble I call upon you, for you answer me.

PSALM 86:5–7 ESV

The Word became a human and lived among us. We saw his glory—the glory that belongs to the only Son of the Father—and he was full of grace and truth. John tells the truth about him and cries out, saying, "This is the One I told you about: 'The One who comes after me is greater than I am, because he was living before me.'" Because he was full of grace and truth, from him we all received one gift after another. The law was given through Moses, but grace and truth came through Jesus Christ. No one has ever seen God. But God the only Son is very close to the Father, and he has shown us what God is like.

JOHN 1:14–18 NCV

All the believers were one in heart and mind. No one
claimed that any of their possessions was their own, but they
shared everything they had. With great power the apostles
continued to testify to the resurrection of the Lord Jesus.
And God's grace was so powerfully at work in them all
that there were no needy persons among them.

ACTS 4:32–34 NIV

The curse of the LORD is on the house of the wicked,
but He blesses the dwelling of the righteous. Though
He scoffs at the scoffers, yet He gives grace to the afflicted.
The wise will inherit honor, but fools display dishonor.

PROVERBS 3:33–35 NASB

The news about them reached the ears of the church
at Jerusalem, and they sent Barnabas off to Antioch.
Then when he arrived and witnessed the grace of God,
he rejoiced and began to encourage them all with resolute
heart to remain true to the Lord; for he was a good man,
and full of the Holy Spirit and of faith. And considerable
numbers were brought to the Lord.

ACTS 11:22–24 NASB

It is the same today, for a few of the people of Israel have remained faithful because of God's grace—his undeserved kindness in choosing them. And since it is through God's kindness, then it is not by their good works. For in that case, God's grace would not be what it really is—free and undeserved.

ROMANS 11:5–6 NLT

"When you go through deep waters, I will be with you. When you go through rivers of difficulty, you will not drown. When you walk through the fire of oppression, you will not be burned up; the flames will not consume you."

ISAIAH 43:2 NLT

However, I consider my life worth nothing to me; my only aim is to finish the race and complete the task the Lord Jesus has given me—the task of testifying to the good news of God's grace.

ACTS 20:24 NIV

As God's co-workers we urge you not to receive God's grace in vain. For he says, "In the time of my favor I heard you, and in the day of salvation I helped you." I tell you, now is the time of God's favor, now is the day of salvation.

2 CORINTHIANS 6:1–2 NIV

God, by his grace through Christ, called you to become his people. So I am amazed that you are turning away so quickly and believing something different than the Good News. Really, there is no other Good News. But some people are confusing you; they want to change the Good News of Christ.

GALATIANS 1:6–7 NCV

My old self has been crucified with Christ. It is no longer I who live, but Christ lives in me. So I live in this earthly body by trusting in the Son of God, who loved me and gave himself for me. I do not treat the grace of God as meaningless. For if keeping the law could make us right with God, then there was no need for Christ to die.

GALATIANS 2:20–21 NLT

Because of the service by which you have proved yourselves,
others will praise God for the obedience that accompanies
your confession of the gospel of Christ, and for your
generosity in sharing with them and with everyone else.
And in their prayers for you their hearts will go out
to you, because of the surpassing grace God has given you.
Thanks be to God for his indescribable gift!

2 CORINTHIANS 9:13–15 NIV

Because of his love, God had already decided to make
us his own children through Jesus Christ. That was what
he wanted and what pleased him, and it brings praise to God
because of his wonderful grace. God gave that grace to us
freely, in Christ, the One he loves. In Christ we are set free
by the blood of his death, and so we have forgiveness of sins.
How rich is God's grace, which he has given to us so fully
and freely. God, with full wisdom and understanding,
let us know his secret purpose. This was what God wanted,
and he planned to do it through Christ.

EPHESIANS 1:5–9 NCV

Everyday Hope

Hope isn't just an emotion; it's a perspective, a discipline, a way of life. Hope is a journey of choice. For believers, hope is vital to a dynamic, thriving faith. . .one of the big three that will remain to the end of time: faith, hope, and love (1 Corinthians 13:13).

Hope is a glimmer in the darkness, that supernatural nudge to persevere when all seems lost. Hope is simply Jesus. May you draw closer to Him as you read through these precious promises from God's Word.

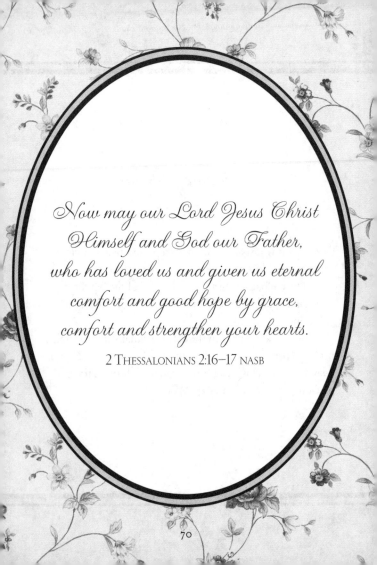

Now may our Lord Jesus Christ
Himself and God our Father,
who has loved us and given us eternal
comfort and good hope by grace,
comfort and strengthen your hearts.

2 THESSALONIANS 2:16–17 NASB

But the LORD looks after those who fear him,
those who put their hope in his love. He saves them
from death and spares their lives in times of hunger.
PSALM 33:18–19 NCV

You are joined together with peace through the Spirit,
so make every effort to continue together in this way. There
is one body and one Spirit, and God called you to have one
hope. There is one Lord, one faith, and one baptism.
EPHESIANS 4:3–5 NCV

Blessed be the God and Father of our Lord Jesus Christ,
who according to His great mercy has caused us to be born
again to a living hope through the resurrection of Jesus Christ
from the dead, to obtain an inheritance which is imperishable
and undefiled and will not fade away, reserved in heaven for
you, who are protected by the power of God through faith
for a salvation ready to be revealed in the last time.
1 PETER 1:3–5 NASB

It teaches us not to live against God nor to do the evil
things the world wants to do. Instead, that grace teaches
us to live now in the present age in a wise and right way
and in a way that shows we serve God. We should live like
that while we wait for our great hope and the coming of
the glory of our great God and Savior Jesus Christ.

TITUS 2:12–13 NCV

We always thank God for all of you and pray for you
constantly. As we pray to our God and Father about you,
we think of your faithful work, your loving deeds, and the
enduring hope you have because of our Lord Jesus Christ.

1 THESSALONIANS 1:2–3 NLT

But we have the true hope that comes from being made right
with God, and by the Spirit we wait eagerly for this hope.

GALATIANS 5:5 NCV

May the God of hope fill you with all joy and peace
as you trust in him, so that you may overflow
with hope by the power of the Holy Spirit.
ROMANS 15:13 NIV

I keep the LORD before me always. Because he is close
by my side, I will not be hurt. So I rejoice and am glad.
Even my body has hope, because you will not leave me
in the grave. You will not let your holy one rot.
PSALM 16:8–10 NCV

But this I call to mind, and therefore I have hope: The
steadfast love of the LORD never ceases; his mercies never
come to an end; they are new every morning; great is
your faithfulness. "The LORD is my portion," says my soul,
"therefore I will hope in him." The LORD is good to
those who wait for him, to the soul who seeks him.
LAMENTATIONS 3:21–25 ESV

But as for me, I watch in hope for the LORD,
I wait for God my Savior; my God will hear me.
MICAH 7:7 NIV

Therefore, since we have been justified through faith, we have peace with God through our Lord Jesus Christ, through whom we have gained access by faith into this grace in which we now stand. And we boast in the hope of the glory of God. Not only so, but we also glory in our sufferings, because we know that suffering produces perseverance; perseverance, character; and character, hope. And hope does not put us to shame, because God's love has been poured out into our hearts through the Holy Spirit, who has been given to us.

ROMANS 5:1–5 NIV

Instead, you must worship Christ as Lord of your life. And if someone asks about your Christian hope, always be ready to explain it.

1 PETER 3:15 NLT

"I am coming to you now, but I say these things while I am still in the world, so that they may have the full measure of my joy within them."

JOHN 17:13 NIV

And we believers also groan, even though we have the Holy
Spirit within us as a foretaste of future glory, for we long for
our bodies to be released from sin and suffering. We, too, wait
with eager hope for the day when God will give us our full
rights as his adopted children, including the new bodies he has
promised us. We were given this hope when we were saved.
(If we already have something, we don't need to hope for it.
But if we look forward to something we don't yet have,
we must wait patiently and confidently.)
ROMANS 8:23–25 NLT

That is what the Scriptures mean when God told him,
"I have made you the father of many nations." This happened
because Abraham believed in the God who brings the dead
back to life and who creates new things out of nothing. Even
when there was no reason for hope, Abraham kept hoping—
believing that he would become the father of many nations.
For God had said to him, "That's how many descendants you
will have!" And Abraham's faith did not weaken, even though,
at about 100 years of age, he figured his body was as good
as dead—and so was Sarah's womb.
ROMANS 4:17–19 NLT

In him we were also chosen, having been predestined according to the plan of him who works out everything in conformity with the purpose of his will, in order that we, who were the first to put our hope in Christ, might be for the praise of his glory. And you also were included in Christ when you heard the message of truth, the gospel of your salvation. When you believed, you were marked in him with a seal, the promised Holy Spirit, who is a deposit guaranteeing our inheritance until the redemption of those who are God's possession—to the praise of his glory.

EPHESIANS 1:11–14 NIV

I trust in you; do not let me be put to shame, nor let my enemies triumph over me. No one who hopes in you will ever be put to shame, but shame will come on those who are treacherous without cause. Show me your ways, LORD, teach me your paths.

PSALM 25:2–4 NIV

But as for me, I will hope continually, and will praise
You yet more and more. My mouth shall tell of Your
righteousness and of Your salvation all day long;
for I do not know the sum of them.
PSALM 71:14–15 NASB

But now he has reconciled you by Christ's physical body
through death to present you holy in his sight, without
blemish and free from accusation—if you continue in your
faith, established and firm, and do not move from the hope
held out in the gospel. This is the gospel that you heard and
that has been proclaimed to every creature under heaven,
and of which I, Paul, have become a servant.
COLOSSIANS 1:22–23 NIV

Those who sleep, sleep at night. Those who get drunk,
get drunk at night. But we belong to the day, so we
should control ourselves. We should wear faith and
love to protect us, and the hope of salvation should
be our helmet. God did not choose us to suffer his anger
but to have salvation through our Lord Jesus Christ.
1 THESSALONIANS 5:7–9 NCV

Love the LORD, all his faithful people! The LORD preserves
those who are true to him, but the proud he pays back in full.
Be strong and take heart, all you who hope in the LORD.
PSALM 31:23–24 NIV

I pray also that you will have greater understanding in your
heart so you will know the hope to which he has called us and
that you will know how rich and glorious are the blessings God
has promised his holy people. And you will know that God's
power is very great for us who believe. That power is the same
as the great strength God used to raise Christ from the dead.
EPHESIANS 1:18–20 NCV

If our hope in Christ is for this life only, we should be
pitied more than anyone else in the world. But Christ
has truly been raised from the dead—the first one and
proof that those who sleep in death will also be raised.
1 CORINTHIANS 15:19–20 NCV

You are my hiding place and my shield;
I hope in your word.
PSALM 119:114 ESV

LORD, sustain me as you promised, that I may live!
Do not let my hope be crushed.
PSALM 119:116 NLT

In the same way, wisdom is sweet to your soul.
If you find it, you will have a bright future,
and your hopes will not be cut short.
PROVERBS 24:14 NLT

Do any of the worthless idols of the nations bring rain?
Do the skies themselves send down showers?
No, it is you, LORD our God. Therefore our hope
is in you, for you are the one who does all this.
JEREMIAH 14:22 NIV

"For I know the plans I have for you," declares the LORD,
"plans to prosper you and not to harm you, plans to give
you hope and a future. Then you will call on me and
come and pray to me, and I will listen to you. You will seek
me and find me when you seek me with all your heart."
JEREMIAH 29:11–13 NIV

This message is the secret that was hidden from everyone since the beginning of time, but now it is made known to God's holy people. God decided to let his people know this rich and glorious secret which he has for all people. This secret is Christ himself, who is in you. He is our only hope for glory.

COLOSSIANS 1:26–27 NCV

Let your unfailing love surround us,
LORD, for our hope is in you alone.

PSALM 33:22 NLT

You have this faith and love because of your hope, and what you hope for is kept safe for you in heaven. You learned about this hope when you heard the message about the truth, the Good News that was told to you. Everywhere in the world that Good News is bringing blessings and is growing. This has happened with you, too, since you heard the Good News and understood the truth about the grace of God.

COLOSSIANS 1:5–6 NCV

Everyday Joy

Is it really possible to have joy in your everyday life—even when the bills are piling up. . .even when you're overwhelmed with work or struggling with emotional problems? Can you truly "rejoice and be glad" in the middle of life's trials? Of course you can! Joy is a choice, and it's one the Lord hopes you'll make in every situation.

God's Word has a lot to say about joy. Read on, and allow the joy of the Lord to seep into your heart and give you just the encouragement and strength you need. Rejoice!

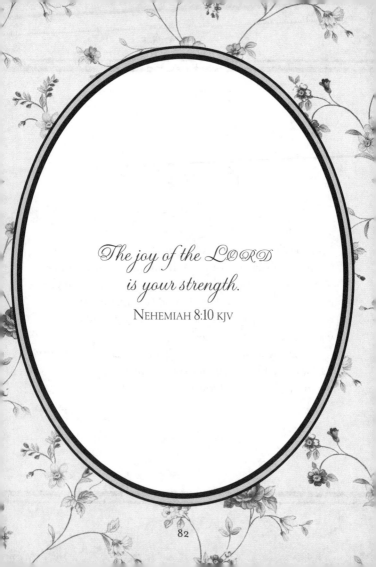

The joy of the LORD
is your strength.

NEHEMIAH 8:10 KJV

Though you have not seen him, you love him; and even though you do not see him now, you believe in him and are filled with an inexpressible and glorious joy, for you are receiving the end result of your faith, the salvation of your souls.

1 Peter 1:8–9 niv

You have turned my mourning into joyful dancing. You have taken away my clothes of mourning and clothed me with joy, that I might sing praises to you and not be silent. O Lord my God, I will give you thanks forever!

Psalm 30:11–12 nlt

Satisfy us in the morning with your unfailing love, that we may sing for joy and be glad all our days.

Psalm 90:14 niv

You make known to me the path of life; you will fill me with joy in your presence, with eternal pleasures at your right hand.

Psalm 16:11 niv

Dear brothers and sisters, when troubles come your way, consider it an opportunity for great joy. For you know that when your faith is tested, your endurance has a chance to grow.

James 1:2–3 nlt

My friends, do not be surprised at the terrible trouble which
now comes to test you. Do not think that something strange
is happening to you. But be happy that you are sharing in
Christ's sufferings so that you will be happy and full of joy
when Christ comes again in glory. When people insult
you because you follow Christ, you are blessed, because the
glorious Spirit, the Spirit of God, is with you.

1 PETER 4:12–14 NCV

Now all glory to God, who is able to keep you from
falling away and will bring you with great joy into
his glorious presence without a single fault.

JUDE 1:24 NLT

Dear brothers and sisters, I close my letter with these
last words: Be joyful. Grow to maturity. Encourage each
other. Live in harmony and peace. Then the God
of love and peace will be with you.

2 CORINTHIANS 13:11 NLT

Be full of joy in the Lord always. I will say again,
be full of joy. Let everyone see that you are
gentle and kind. The Lord is coming soon.

PHILIPPIANS 4:4–5 NCV

And so, from the day we heard, we have not ceased to pray
for you, asking that you may be filled with the knowledge
of his will in all spiritual wisdom and understanding, so as
to walk in a manner worthy of the Lord, fully pleasing to
him, bearing fruit in every good work and increasing in the
knowledge of God. May you be strengthened with all power,
according to his glorious might, for all endurance and patience
with joy, giving thanks to the Father, who has qualified
you to share in the inheritance of the saints in light.

COLOSSIANS 1:9–12 ESV

For the Kingdom of God is not a matter of what we eat
or drink, but of living a life of goodness and peace and joy
in the Holy Spirit. If you serve Christ with this attitude,
you will please God, and others will approve of you, too.

ROMANS 14:17–18 NLT

"When he arrives, he will call together his friends and neighbors, saying, 'Rejoice with me because I have found my lost sheep.' In the same way, there is more joy in heaven over one lost sinner who repents and returns to God than over ninety-nine others who are righteous and haven't strayed away!"

LUKE 15:6–7 NLT

"If you keep my commands, you will remain in my love, just as I have kept my Father's commands and remain in his love. I have told you this so that my joy may be in you and that your joy may be complete. My command is this: Love each other as I have loved you."

JOHN 15:10–12 NIV

For I know the thoughts that I think toward you, says the Lord, thoughts of peace and not of evil, to give you a future and a hope.

JEREMIAH 29:11 NKJV

"You haven't done this before. Ask, using my name, and you will receive, and you will have abundant joy."

JOHN 16:24 NLT

Light shines on the godly, and joy on those whose hearts are right. May all who are godly rejoice in the LORD and praise his holy name!

PSALM 97:11–12 NLT

Shout with joy to the LORD, all the earth! Worship the LORD with gladness. Come before him, singing with joy. Acknowledge that the LORD is God! He made us, and we are his. We are his people, the sheep of his pasture.

PSALM 100:1–3 NLT

So be truly glad. There is wonderful joy ahead, even though you have to endure many trials for a little while. These trials will show that your faith is genuine. It is being tested as fire tests and purifies gold—though your faith is far more precious than mere gold. So when your faith remains strong through many trials, it will bring you much praise and glory and honor on the day when Jesus Christ is revealed to the whole world.

1 PETER 1:6–7 NLT

And you became like us and like the Lord.
You suffered much, but still you accepted the teaching
with the joy that comes from the Holy Spirit.
1 THESSALONIANS 1:6 NCV

For they disciplined us for a short time as seemed best to
them, but He disciplines us for our good, so that we may share
His holiness. All discipline for the moment seems not to be
joyful, but sorrowful; yet to those who have been trained by it,
afterwards it yields the peaceful fruit of righteousness.
HEBREWS 12:10–11 NASB

Therefore you too have grief now;
but I will see you again, and your heart will rejoice,
and no one will take your joy away from you.
JOHN 16:22 NASB

But the angel said to them, "Do not be afraid. I bring
you good news that will cause great joy for all the
people. Today in the town of David a Savior has been
born to you; he is the Messiah, the Lord."
LUKE 2:10–11 NIV

A joyful heart is good medicine,
but a crushed spirit dries up the bones.
PROVERBS 17:22 ESV

When I discovered your words, I devoured them.
They are my joy and my heart's delight, for I bear
your name, O LORD God of Heaven's Armies.
JEREMIAH 15:16 NLT

When I said, "My foot is slipping," your unfailing love,
LORD, supported me. When anxiety was great within me,
your consolation brought me joy.
PSALM 94:18–19 NIV

Our mouths were filled with laughter, our tongues
with songs of joy. Then it was said among the nations,
"The LORD has done great things for them." The LORD
has done great things for us, and we are filled with joy.
PSALM 126:2–3 NIV

God places the lonely in families;
he sets the prisoners free and gives them joy.
PSALM 68:6 NLT

Purify me from my sins, and I will be clean; wash me, and I will be whiter than snow. Oh, give me back my joy again; you have broken me—now let me rejoice.

PSALM 51:7–8 NLT

But as for me, I shall sing of Your strength; yes, I shall joyfully sing of Your lovingkindness in the morning, for You have been my stronghold and a refuge in the day of my distress. O my strength, I will sing praises to You; for God is my stronghold, the God who shows me lovingkindness.

PSALM 59:16–17 NASB

Shout for joy to God, all the earth!
Sing the glory of his name; make his praise glorious.

PSALM 66:1–2 NIV

For the angel of the LORD is a guard; he surrounds and defends all who fear him. Taste and see that the LORD is good. Oh, the joys of those who take refuge in him!

PSALM 34:7–8 NLT

How lovely are Your dwelling places, O LORD of hosts!
My soul longed and even yearned for the courts of the LORD;
my heart and my flesh sing for joy to the living God.
PSALM 84:1–2 NASB

For You, O LORD, have made me glad by what You
have done, I will sing for joy at the works of Your hands.
PSALM 92:4 NASB

Sing to the LORD, all you godly ones! Praise his holy
name. For his anger lasts only a moment, but his favor
lasts a lifetime! Weeping may last through the night,
but joy comes with the morning.
PSALM 30:4–5 NLT

I will praise you, LORD, with all my heart; I will tell of all the
marvelous things you have done. I will be filled with joy because
of you. I will sing praises to your name, O Most High.
PSALM 9:1–2 NLT

"I take joy in doing your will, my God,
for your instructions are written on my heart."
PSALM 40:8 NLT

But may all who search for you be filled with
joy and gladness in you. May those who love your
salvation repeatedly shout, "The LORD is great!"
PSALM 40:16 NLT

Get rid of all bitterness, rage, anger, harsh words,
and slander, as well as all types of evil behavior. Instead,
be kind to each other, tenderhearted, forgiving one another,
just as God through Christ has forgiven you.
EPHESIANS 4:31–32 NLT

So rejoice in the LORD and be glad, all you who obey him!
Shout for joy, all you whose hearts are pure!
PSALM 32:11 NLT

Everyday Love

Love is one of those words that we use all the time—and often out of context. We say, "I love this pizza!" or "I love that TV show!" But when it comes to loving people, well, that's quite a bit harder. It's tough to love others when they're not treating us as they should. And it's even harder when the wounds run deep.

Thankfully, God shows us, through His Word, how to love even the most unlovable person. And He reveals His great love for us within the scriptures as well. Praise Him for His wondrous love!

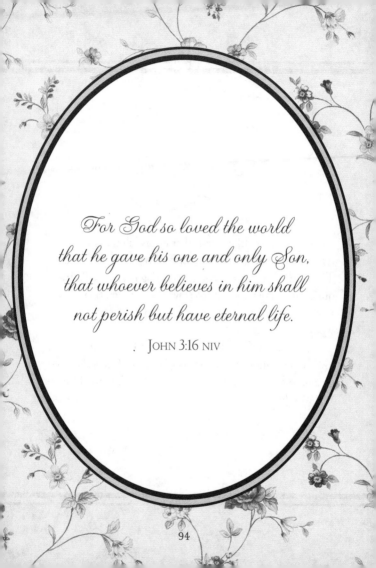

For God so loved the world
that he gave his one and only Son,
that whoever believes in him shall
not perish but have eternal life.

JOHN 3:16 NIV

If I speak in the tongues of men or of angels, but do not have love, I am only a resounding gong or a clanging cymbal. If I have the gift of prophecy and can fathom all mysteries and all knowledge, and if I have a faith that can move mountains, but do not have love, I am nothing. If I give all I possess to the poor and give over my body to hardship that I may boast, but do not have love, I gain nothing.

1 CORINTHIANS 13:1–3 NIV

Don't just pretend to love others. Really love them. Hate what is wrong. Hold tightly to what is good. Love each other with genuine affection, and take delight in honoring each other.

ROMANS 12:9–10 NLT

Jesus replied, "Anyone who loves me will obey my teaching. My Father will love them, and we will come to them and make our home with them."

JOHN 14:23 NIV

"This is my commandment, that you love one another as I have loved you. Greater love has no one than this, that someone lay down his life for his friends."

JOHN 15:12–13 ESV

Love is patient, love is kind. It does not envy, it does not boast, it is not proud. It does not dishonor others, it is not self-seeking, it is not easily angered, it keeps no record of wrongs. Love does not delight in evil but rejoices with the truth. It always protects, always trusts, always hopes, always perseveres. Love never fails.

1 CORINTHIANS 13:4–8 NIV

"A new commandment I give to you, that you love one another: just as I have loved you, you also are to love one another. By this all people will know that you are my disciples, if you have love for one another."

JOHN 13:34–35 ESV

Let love and faithfulness never leave you; bind them around your neck, write them on the tablet of your heart. Then you will win favor and a good name in the sight of God and man.

PROVERBS 3:3–4 NIV

And I am convinced that nothing can ever separate us from God's love. Neither death nor life, neither angels nor demons, neither our fears for today nor our worries about tomorrow— not even the powers of hell can separate us from God's love. No power in the sky above or in the earth below—indeed, nothing in all creation will ever be able to separate us from the love of God that is revealed in Christ Jesus our Lord.

ROMANS 8:38–39 NLT

"For the Father himself loves you, because you have loved me and have believed that I came from God. I came from the Father and have come into the world, and now I am leaving the world and going to the Father. . . . I have said these things to you, that in me you may have peace. In the world you will have tribulation. But take heart; I have overcome the world."

JOHN 16:27–28, 33 ESV

"You did not choose me, but I chose you and appointed
you that you should go and bear fruit and that your fruit
should abide, so that whatever you ask the Father in my
name, he may give it to you. These things I command
you, so that you will love one another."

JOHN 15:16–17 ESV

Whoever does not love does not know God,
because God is love. This is how God showed his
love among us: He sent his one and only Son into
the world that we might live through him.

1 JOHN 4:8–9 NIV

But because of his great love for us, God, who is rich
in mercy, made us alive with Christ even when we were
dead in transgressions—it is by grace you have been saved.

EPHESIANS 2:4–5 NIV

Dear friends, let us continue to love one another,
for love comes from God. Anyone who loves is a
child of God and knows God. But anyone who
does not love does not know God, for God is love.

1 JOHN 4:7–8 NLT

You, my brothers and sisters, were called to be free. But do not use your freedom to indulge the flesh; rather, serve one another humbly in love. For the entire law is fulfilled in keeping this one command: "Love your neighbor as yourself."
GALATIANS 5:13–14 NIV

"If you keep my commandments, you will abide in my love, just as I have kept my Father's commandments and abide in his love. These things I have spoken to you, that my joy may be in you, and that your joy may be full."
JOHN 15:10–11 ESV

For you bless the godly, O LORD;
you surround them with your shield of love.
PSALM 5:12 NLT

Return, O LORD, and rescue me.
Save me because of your unfailing love.
PSALM 6:4 NLT

Because of your unfailing love, I can enter your house;
I will worship at your Temple with deepest awe. Lead
me in the right path, O LORD, or my enemies will
conquer me. Make your way plain for me to follow.
PSALM 5:7–8 NLT

I am praying to you because I know you will answer, O God.
Bend down and listen as I pray. Show me your unfailing love
in wonderful ways. By your mighty power you rescue those
who seek refuge from their enemies. Guard me as you would
guard your own eyes. Hide me in the shadow of your wings.
PSALM 17:6–8 NLT

"Teacher, which is the greatest commandment in the
Law?" Jesus replied: " 'Love the Lord your God with
all your heart and with all your soul and with all your
mind.' This is the first and greatest commandment.
And the second is like it: 'Love your neighbor as yourself.'"
MATTHEW 22:36–39 NIV

"But love your enemies, and do good, and lend,
expecting nothing in return; and your reward will
be great, and you will be sons of the Most High;
for He Himself is kind to ungrateful and evil men.
Be merciful, just as your Father is merciful."
LUKE 6:35–36 NASB

So the Word became human and made his home among us.
He was full of unfailing love and faithfulness. And we have
seen his glory, the glory of the Father's one and only Son.
JOHN 1:14 NLT

This is how God showed his love to us:
He sent his one and only Son into the world
so that we could have life through him.
1 JOHN 4:9 NCV

We have confidence in the Lord that you are
doing and will continue to do the things we
command. May the Lord direct your hearts
into God's love and Christ's perseverance.
2 THESSALONIANS 3:4–5 NIV

Praise the LORD, all nations! Extol him, all peoples!
For great is his steadfast love toward us, and the
faithfulness of the LORD endures forever. Praise the LORD!
PSALM 117:1–2 ESV

Many waters cannot quench love;
rivers cannot sweep it away.
SONG OF SONGS 8:7 NIV

"You have heard that it was said, 'You shall love your
neighbor and hate your enemy.' But I say to you,
Love your enemies and pray for those who persecute
you, so that you may be sons of your Father who is in
heaven. For he makes his sun rise on the evil and on the
good, and sends rain on the just and on the unjust."
MATTHEW 5:43–45 ESV

Those who are wise will take all this to heart;
they will see in our history the faithful love of the LORD.
PSALM 107:43 NLT

"Whoever has my commands and keeps them is the one who loves me. The one who loves me will be loved by my Father, and I too will love them and show myself to them."

JOHN 14:21 NIV

And this hope will not lead to disappointment. For we know how dearly God loves us, because he has given us the Holy Spirit to fill our hearts with his love.

ROMANS 5:5 NLT

But the LORD watches over those who fear him, those who rely on his unfailing love. He rescues them from death and keeps them alive in times of famine. We put our hope in the LORD. He is our help and our shield. In him our hearts rejoice, for we trust in his holy name. Let your unfailing love surround us, LORD, for our hope is in you alone.

PSALM 33:18–22 NLT

I will be glad and rejoice in your love, for you saw
my affliction and knew the anguish of my soul.
You have not given me into the hands of the enemy
but have set my feet in a spacious place.
PSALM 31:7–8 NIV

I will sing of the LORD's great love forever; with my mouth
I will make your faithfulness known through all generations.
I will declare that your love stands firm forever, that you
have established your faithfulness in heaven itself.
PSALM 89:1–2 NIV

Be on your guard; stand firm in the faith;
be courageous; be strong. Do everything in love.
1 CORINTHIANS 16:13–14 NIV

I have been crucified with Christ. It is no longer
I who live, but Christ who lives in me. And the life
I now live in the flesh I live by faith in the Son of God,
who loved me and gave himself for me.
GALATIANS 2:20 ESV

Everyday Peace

God sent His Son, Jesus, into the world to bring you genuine and lasting peace. Through His power to renew and restore, He eases your anxieties with the balm of forgiveness. He opens the way to a loving and sustaining relationship with your heavenly Father. With His Spirit alive in your heart, He gently leads you to His stillness.

These Bible promises will offer support and encouragement as you reach out to God for serenity of heart, mind, and spirit. Lean on the One who is Peace, and you'll discover that serenity is available, achievable, and yours.

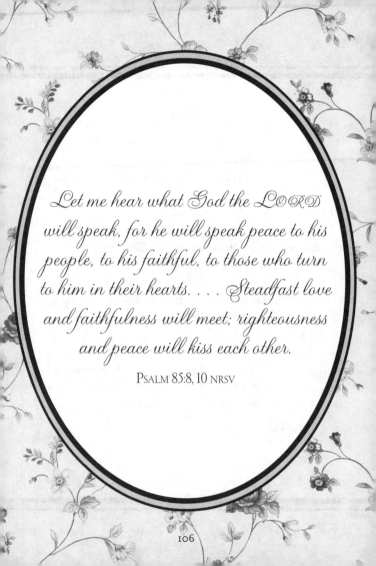

Let me hear what God the LORD will speak, for he will speak peace to his people, to his faithful, to those who turn to him in their hearts. . . . Steadfast love and faithfulness will meet; righteousness and peace will kiss each other.

PSALM 85:8, 10 NRSV

And let the peace that comes from Christ rule in your hearts.
For as members of one body you are called to live in peace.
And always be thankful.
COLOSSIANS 3:15 NLT

God is our refuge and strength, always ready to help
in times of trouble. So we will not fear when earthquakes
come and the mountains crumble into the sea.
PSALM 46:1–2 NLT

The law of Moses was unable to save us because of the
weakness of our sinful nature. So God did what the law could
not do. He sent his own Son in a body like the bodies we
sinners have. And in that body God declared an end to sin's
control over us by giving his Son as a sacrifice for our sins.
ROMANS 8:3 NLT

Many people say, "Who will show us better times?"
Let your face smile on us, LORD. You have given me
greater joy than those who have abundant harvests of
grain and new wine. In peace I will lie down and sleep,
for you alone, O LORD, will keep me safe.

PSALM 4:6–8 NLT

Do not repay anyone evil for evil. Be careful to do what
is right in the eyes of everyone. If it is possible, as far as it
depends on you, live at peace with everyone. Do not take
revenge, my dear friends, but leave room for God's wrath, for it
is written: "It is mine to avenge; I will repay," says the Lord.

ROMANS 12:17–19 NIV

So then we pursue the things which make
for peace and the building up of one another.

ROMANS 14:19 NASB

"May the Lord bless you and keep you. May the
Lord show you his kindness and have mercy on you.
May the Lord watch over you and give you peace."

NUMBERS 6:24–26 NCV

For God is not a God of confusion but of peace,
as in all the churches of the saints.
1 CORINTHIANS 14:33 NASB

"Blessed are the peacemakers,
for they will be called children of God."
MATTHEW 5:9 NRSV

No discipline seems pleasant at the time, but painful.
Later on, however, it produces a harvest of righteousness
and peace for those who have been trained by it.
HEBREWS 12:11 NIV

But the wisdom that comes from heaven is first of all pure;
then peace-loving, considerate, submissive, full of mercy
and good fruit, impartial and sincere. Peacemakers who
sow in peace reap a harvest of righteousness.
JAMES 3:17–18 NIV

May God himself, the God of peace, sanctify you through
and through. May your whole spirit, soul and body be
kept blameless at the coming of our Lord Jesus Christ.
The one who calls you is faithful, and he will do it.
1 THESSALONIANS 5:23–24 NIV

Therefore, if anyone cleanses himself from what is
dishonorable, he will be a vessel for honorable use,
set apart as holy, useful to the master of the house,
ready for every good work. So flee youthful passions
and pursue righteousness, faith, love, and peace,
along with those who call on the Lord from a pure heart.
2 TIMOTHY 2:21–22 ESV

For God was pleased to have all his fullness dwell in him,
and through him to reconcile to himself all things,
whether things on earth or things in heaven,
by making peace through his blood, shed on the cross.
COLOSSIANS 1:19–20 NIV

Those who live according to the flesh have their minds
set on what the flesh desires; but those who live in accordance
with the Spirit have their minds set on what the Spirit desires.
The mind governed by the flesh is death, but the mind
governed by the Spirit is life and peace.

ROMANS 8:5–6 NIV

But now in Christ Jesus you who once were far away have
been brought near by the blood of Christ. For he himself
is our peace, who has made the two groups one and has
destroyed the barrier, the dividing wall of hostility, by setting
aside in his flesh the law with its commands and regulations.
His purpose was to create in himself one new humanity out
of the two, thus making peace, and in one body to reconcile
both of them to God through the cross, by which he put to
death their hostility. He came and preached peace to you who
were far away and peace to those who were near. For through
him we both have access to the Father by one Spirit.

EPHESIANS 2:13–18 NIV

Be completely humble and gentle; be patient, bearing with one another in love. Make every effort to keep the unity of the Spirit through the bond of peace. There is one body and one Spirit, just as you were called to one hope when you were called; one Lord, one faith, one baptism; one God and Father of all, who is over all and through all and in all.

EPHESIANS 4:2–6 NIV

Now we ask you, brothers and sisters, to acknowledge those who work hard among you, who care for you in the Lord and who admonish you. Hold them in the highest regard in love because of their work. Live in peace with each other. And we urge you, brothers and sisters, warn those who are idle and disruptive, encourage the disheartened, help the weak, be patient with everyone.

1 THESSALONIANS 5:12–14 NIV

"Peace I leave with you; my peace I give you.
I do not give to you as the world gives. Do not
let your hearts be troubled and do not be afraid."

JOHN 14:27 NIV

Finally, beloved, whatever is true, whatever is honorable, whatever is just, whatever is pure, whatever is pleasing, whatever is commendable, if there is any excellence and if there is anything worthy of praise, think about these things. Keep on doing the things that you have learned and received and heard and seen in me, and the God of peace will be with you.
PHILIPPIANS 4:8–9 NRSV

Deceit is in the hearts of those who plot evil,
but those who promote peace have joy.
PROVERBS 12:20 NIV

When a man's ways are pleasing to the LORD,
He makes even his enemies to be at peace with him.
PROVERBS 16:7 NASB

But the LORD sits enthroned forever; he has established his throne for justice, and he judges the world with righteousness; he judges the peoples with uprightness. The LORD is a stronghold for the oppressed, a stronghold in times of trouble. And those who know your name put their trust in you, for you, O LORD, have not forsaken those who seek you.
PSALM 9:7–10 ESV

Seven times a day I praise You, because of Your righteous ordinances. Those who love Your law have great peace, and nothing causes them to stumble. I hope for Your salvation, O LORD, and do Your commandments.
PSALM 119:164–166 NASB

You keep him in perfect peace whose mind is stayed on you, because he trusts in you. Trust in the LORD forever, for the LORD GOD is an everlasting rock.
ISAIAH 26:3–4 ESV

You are my hiding place; you will protect me from trouble and surround me with songs of deliverance. I will instruct you and teach you in the way you should go; I will counsel you with my loving eye on you. . . . Many are the woes of the wicked, but the LORD's unfailing love surrounds the one who trusts in him. Rejoice in the LORD and be glad, you righteous; sing, all you who are upright in heart!
PSALM 32:7–8, 10–11 NIV

Come, my children, listen to me; I will teach you the fear of the LORD. Whoever of you loves life and desires to see many good days, keep your tongue from evil and your lips from telling lies. Turn from evil and do good; seek peace and pursue it.

PSALM 34:11–14 NIV

A little while, and the wicked will be no more; though you look for them, they will not be found. But the meek will inherit the land and enjoy peace and prosperity.

PSALM 37:10–11 NIV

Honor the LORD, you heavenly beings; honor the LORD for his glory and strength. Honor the LORD for the glory of his name. Worship the LORD in the splendor of his holiness. . . . The LORD gives his people strength. The LORD blesses them with peace.

PSALM 29:1–2, 11 NLT

Consider the blameless, observe the upright; a future awaits those who seek peace.

PSALM 37:37 NIV

Don't worry about anything; instead, pray about everything.
Tell God what you need, and thank him for all he has done.
Then you will experience God's peace, which exceeds anything
we can understand. His peace will guard your hearts
and minds as you live in Christ Jesus.

PHILIPPIANS 4:6–7 NLT

Suddenly a great company of the heavenly host
appeared with the angel, praising God and saying,
"Glory to God in the highest heaven, and on
earth peace to those on whom his favor rests."

LUKE 2:13–14 NIV

But let all who take refuge in you be glad; let them ever sing for
joy. Spread your protection over them, that those who love your
name may rejoice in you. Surely, LORD, you bless the righteous;
you surround them with your favor as with a shield.

PSALM 5:11–12 NIV

Everyday Praise

As women, we can learn a lot about passion, emotion, and praise through the poetry of the book of Psalms. The psalms were composed by at least six authors—perhaps more— and they were nothing if not real. They cried out to God unabashed, and their prayers seem to put our own struggles into words.

Draw closer to the heavenly Father as you read through these Bible promises, for He alone offers help, hope, and healing to your spirit. Praise Him!

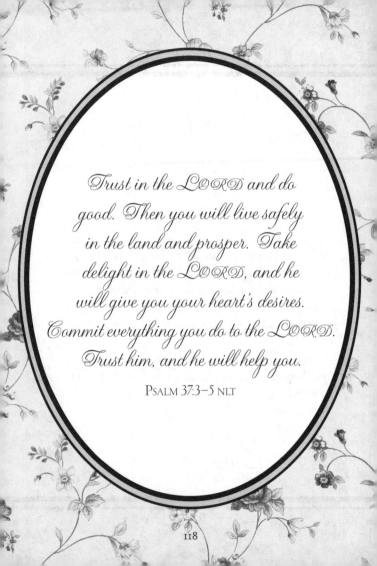

Trust in the LORD and do good. Then you will live safely in the land and prosper. Take delight in the LORD, and he will give you your heart's desires. Commit everything you do to the LORD. Trust him, and he will help you.

Psalm 37:3–5 NLT

I will give thanks to you, LORD, with all my heart; I will tell of all your wonderful deeds. I will be glad and rejoice in you; I will sing the praises of your name, O Most High.

PSALM 9:1–2 NIV

I will praise the LORD, who counsels me; even at night my heart instructs me. I keep my eyes always on the LORD. With him at my right hand, I will not be shaken.

PSALM 16:7–8 NIV

The LORD is my rock and my fortress and my deliverer, my God, my rock, in whom I take refuge; my shield and the horn of my salvation, my stronghold. I call upon the LORD, who is worthy to be praised, and I am saved from my enemies.

PSALM 18:2–3 NASB

I praise you, for I am fearfully and wonderfully made. Wonderful are your works; that I know very well.

PSALM 139:14 NRSV

Praise the LORD! How good it is to sing praises to our God; for he is gracious, and a song of praise is fitting.... He heals the brokenhearted, and binds up their wounds.

PSALM 147:1, 3 NRSV

I will bow down toward your holy temple and will praise your name for your unfailing love and your faithfulness, for you have so exalted your solemn decree that it surpasses your fame. When I called, you answered me; you greatly emboldened me.

PSALM 138:2–3 NIV

Save us, LORD our God, and gather us from the nations, that we may give thanks to your holy name and glory in your praise. Praise be to the LORD, the God of Israel, from everlasting to everlasting. Let all the people say, "Amen!" Praise the LORD.

PSALM 106:47–48 NIV

But as for us, we will bless the LORD from this time forth and forever. Praise the LORD!

PSALM 115:18 NASB

Praise the LORD. Praise the LORD, you his servants; praise the name of the LORD. Let the name of the LORD be praised, both now and forevermore. From the rising of the sun to the place where it sets, the name of the LORD is to be praised.

PSALM 113:1–3 NIV

"I am coming to you now, but I say these things while I am still in the world, so that they may have the full measure of my joy within them."

JOHN 17:13 NIV

Oh come, let us sing to the LORD; let us make a joyful noise to the rock of our salvation! Let us come into his presence with thanksgiving; let us make a joyful noise to him with songs of praise! For the LORD is a great God, and a great King above all gods.

PSALM 95:1–3 ESV

Is anyone among you in trouble? Let them pray. Is anyone happy? Let them sing songs of praise.

JAMES 5:13 NIV

Know that the LORD is God. It is he who made us,
and we are his; we are his people, the sheep of his pasture.
Enter his gates with thanksgiving and his courts with praise;
give thanks to him and praise his name. For the LORD
is good and his love endures forever; his faithfulness
continues through all generations.
PSALM 100:3–5 NIV

Praise the LORD, my soul; all my inmost being, praise his
holy name. Praise the LORD, my soul, and forget not all his
benefits—who forgives all your sins and heals all your diseases,
who redeems your life from the pit and crowns you with love
and compassion, who satisfies your desires with good things
so that your youth is renewed like the eagle's.
PSALM 103:1–5 NIV

Praise the LORD! I will give thanks to the LORD with my whole heart, in the company of the upright, in the congregation. Great are the works of the LORD, studied by all who delight in them. Full of splendor and majesty is his work, and his righteousness endures forever.

PSALM 111:1–3 ESV

He has remembered his steadfast love and faithfulness to the house of Israel. All the ends of the earth have seen the salvation of our God. Make a joyful noise to the LORD, all the earth; break forth into joyous song and sing praises! Sing praises to the LORD with the lyre, with the lyre and the sound of melody!

PSALM 98:3–5 ESV

Praise him with clanging cymbals; praise him with loud clashing cymbals! Let everything that breathes praise the LORD! Praise the LORD!

PSALM 150:5–6 NRSV

From you comes the theme of my praise in the great assembly;
before those who fear you I will fulfill my vows. The poor
will eat and be satisfied; those who seek the LORD will praise
him—may your hearts live forever! All the ends of the earth
will remember and turn to the LORD, and all the families of
the nations will bow down before him, for dominion belongs
to the LORD and he rules over the nations.
PSALM 22:25–28 NIV

Praise be to the LORD, for he has heard my cry for mercy.
The LORD is my strength and my shield; my heart
trusts in him, and he helps me. My heart leaps for joy,
and with my song I praise him.
PSALM 28:6–7 NIV

As sorrowful, yet always rejoicing;
as poor, yet making many rich;
as having nothing, and yet possessing all things.
2 CORINTHIANS 6:10 KJV

You have turned for me my mourning into dancing;
You have loosed my sackcloth and girded me with gladness,
that my soul may sing praise to You and not be silent.
O LORD my God, I will give thanks to You forever.
PSALM 30:11–12 NASB

Sing joyfully to the LORD, you righteous; it is fitting for
the upright to praise him. Praise the LORD with the harp;
make music to him on the ten-stringed lyre. Sing to
him a new song; play skillfully, and shout for joy.
PSALM 33:1–3 NIV

I will cause your name to be remembered in all generations;
therefore nations will praise you forever and ever.
PSALM 45:17 ESV

He drew me up from the pit of destruction, out of the miry bog, and set my feet upon a rock, making my steps secure. He put a new song in my mouth, a song of praise to our God. Many will see and fear, and put their trust in the LORD.
PSALM 40:2–3 ESV

Why are you in despair, O my soul? And why have you become disturbed within me? Hope in God, for I shall again praise Him for the help of His presence.
PSALM 42:5 NASB

Sing praises to God, sing praises! Sing praises to our King, sing praises! For God is the King of all the earth; sing praises with a psalm! God reigns over the nations; God sits on his holy throne.
PSALM 47:6–8 ESV

Give praise to the LORD, proclaim his name; make known among the nations what he has done. Sing to him, sing praise to him; tell of all his wonderful acts. Glory in his holy name; let the hearts of those who seek the LORD rejoice.

PSALM 105:1–3 NIV

For you have been my hope, Sovereign LORD, my confidence since my youth. From birth I have relied on you; you brought me forth from my mother's womb. I will ever praise you. I have become a sign to many; you are my strong refuge. My mouth is filled with your praise, declaring your splendor all day long.

PSALM 71:5–8 NIV

I will also praise you with the harp for your faithfulness, O my God; I will sing praises to you with the lyre, O Holy One of Israel. My lips will shout for joy, when I sing praises to you; my soul also, which you have redeemed. And my tongue will talk of your righteous help all the day long, for they have been put to shame and disappointed who sought to do me hurt.

PSALM 71:22–24 ESV

Praise awaits you, our God, in Zion; to you our
vows will be fulfilled. You who answer prayer,
to you all people will come. When we were
overwhelmed by sins, you forgave our transgressions.
PSALM 65:1–3 NIV

Praise be to the LORD God, the God of Israel, who alone does
marvelous deeds. Praise be to his glorious name forever; may
the whole earth be filled with his glory. Amen and Amen.
PSALM 72:18–19 NIV

I will extol you, my God and King, and bless your name
forever and ever. Every day I will bless you, and praise your
name forever and ever. Great is the LORD, and greatly
to be praised; his greatness is unsearchable.
PSALM 145:1–3 NRSV

Everyday Prayers

We are welcome—anytime, 24/7—to converse with the King of the universe. The all-powerful God we serve is interested in each one of us, and He truly cares about what we have to say. That's real, genuine love!

May each of these Bible promises challenge and encourage your spirit as you open your heart to a more intimate relationship with your heavenly Father.

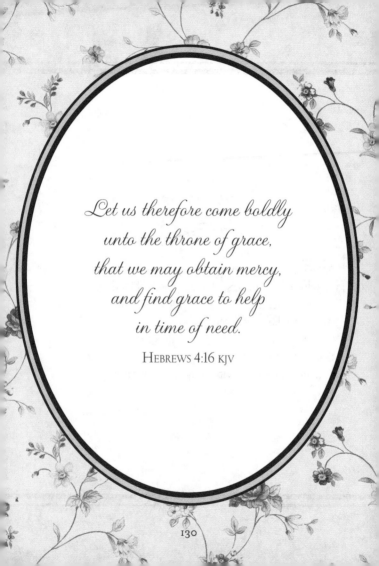

Let us therefore come boldly
unto the throne of grace,
that we may obtain mercy,
and find grace to help
in time of need.

HEBREWS 4:16 KJV

I will praise you, LORD, among the nations; I will sing of you among the peoples. For great is your love, higher than the heavens; your faithfulness reaches to the skies. Be exalted, O God, above the heavens; let your glory be over all the earth.

PSALM 108:3–5 NIV

For this reason I kneel before the Father, from whom every family in heaven and on earth derives its name. I pray that out of his glorious riches he may strengthen you with power through his Spirit in your inner being, so that Christ may dwell in your hearts through faith. And I pray that you, being rooted and established in love, may have power, together with all the Lord's holy people, to grasp how wide and long and high and deep is the love of Christ, and to know this love that surpasses knowledge—that you may be filled to the measure of all the fullness of God. Now to him who is able to do immeasurably more than all we ask or imagine, according to his power that is at work within us, to him be glory in the church and in Christ Jesus throughout all generations, for ever and ever! Amen.

EPHESIANS 3:14–21 NIV

You have searched me, LORD, and you know me.
You know when I sit and when I rise; you perceive my
thoughts from afar. You discern my going out and my lying
down; you are familiar with all my ways. Before a word is on
my tongue you, LORD, know it completely.

PSALM 139:1–4 NIV

Give ear to my words, O LORD, consider my groaning.
Heed the sound of my cry for help, my King and my God,
for to You I pray. In the morning, O LORD, You will hear
my voice; in the morning I will order my prayer
to You and eagerly watch.

PSALM 5:1–3 NASB

I love you, LORD; you are my strength. The LORD is my rock,
my fortress, and my savior; my God is my rock, in whom I
find protection. He is my shield, the power that saves me, and
my place of safety. I called on the LORD, who is worthy of
praise, and he saved me from my enemies.

PSALM 18:1–3 NLT

But I pray to you, LORD, in the time of your favor; in your great love, O God, answer me with your sure salvation. Rescue me from the mire, do not let me sink; deliver me from those who hate me, from the deep waters. Do not let the floodwaters engulf me or the depths swallow me up or the pit close its mouth over me. Answer me, LORD, out of the goodness of your love; in your great mercy turn to me. Do not hide your face from your servant; answer me quickly, for I am in trouble. Come near and rescue me; deliver me because of my foes.

PSALM 69:13–18 NIV

"This, then, is how you should pray: 'Our Father in heaven, hallowed be your name, your kingdom come, your will be done, on earth as it is in heaven. Give us today our daily bread. And forgive us our debts, as we also have forgiven our debtors. And lead us not into temptation, but deliver us from the evil one.'"

MATTHEW 6:9–13 NIV

I prayed to the LORD my God and confessed: "O Lord, you are a great and awesome God! You always fulfill your covenant and keep your promises of unfailing love to those who love you and obey your commands. But we have sinned and done wrong. We have rebelled against you and scorned your commands and regulations. We have refused to listen to your servants the prophets, who spoke on your authority to our kings and princes and ancestors and to all the people of the land. Lord, you are in the right; but as you see, our faces are covered with shame. This is true of all of us, including the people of Judah and Jerusalem and all Israel, scattered near and far, wherever you have driven us because of our disloyalty to you. O LORD, we and our kings, princes, and ancestors are covered with shame because we have sinned against you.

But the Lord our God is merciful and forgiving, even though we have rebelled against him."

DANIEL 9:4–9 NLT

Have mercy on me, O God, according to your unfailing love; according to your great compassion blot out my transgressions. Wash away all my iniquity and cleanse me from my sin. For I know my transgressions, and my sin is always before me. Against you, you only, have I sinned and done what is evil in your sight; so you are right in your verdict and justified when you judge. Surely I was sinful at birth, sinful from the time my mother conceived me. Yet you desired faithfulness even in the womb; you taught me wisdom in that secret place.

PSALM 51:1–6 NIV

LORD, I have heard of your fame; I stand in awe of your deeds, LORD. Repeat them in our day, in our time make them known; in wrath remember mercy. . . . Though the fig tree does not bud and there are no grapes on the vines, though the olive crop fails and the fields produce no food, though there are no sheep in the pen and no cattle in the stalls, yet I will rejoice in the LORD, I will be joyful in God my Savior. The Sovereign LORD is my strength; he makes my feet like the feet of a deer, he enables me to tread on the heights.

HABAKKUK 3:2, 17–19 NIV

Cleanse me with hyssop, and I will be clean; wash me, and I will be whiter than snow. Let me hear joy and gladness; let the bones you have crushed rejoice. Hide your face from my sins and blot out all my iniquity. Create in me a pure heart, O God, and renew a steadfast spirit within me.

Do not cast me from your presence or take your Holy Spirit from me. Restore to me the joy of your salvation and grant me a willing spirit, to sustain me.

PSALM 51:7–12 NIV

LORD, how many are my foes! How many rise up against me! Many are saying of me, "God will not deliver him." But you, LORD, are a shield around me, my glory, the One who lifts my head high. I call out to the LORD, and he answers me from his holy mountain. I lie down and sleep; I wake again, because the LORD sustains me. I will not fear though tens of thousands assail me on every side. Arise, LORD! Deliver me, my God! Strike all my enemies on the jaw; break the teeth of the wicked. From the LORD comes deliverance. May your blessing be on your people.

PSALM 3:1–8 NIV

"Praise be to you, LORD, the God of our father Israel, from everlasting to everlasting. Yours, LORD, is the greatness and the power and the glory and the majesty and the splendor, for everything in heaven and earth is yours. Yours, LORD, is the kingdom; you are exalted as head over all. Wealth and honor come from you; you are the ruler of all things. In your hands are strength and power to exalt and give strength to all. Now, our God, we give you thanks, and praise your glorious name."

1 CHRONICLES 29:10–13 NIV

The LORD is my shepherd, I lack nothing. He makes me lie down in green pastures, he leads me beside quiet waters, he refreshes my soul. He guides me along the right paths for his name's sake. Even though I walk through the darkest valley, I will fear no evil, for you are with me; your rod and your staff, they comfort me. You prepare a table before me in the presence of my enemies. You anoint my head with oil; my cup overflows. Surely your goodness and love will follow me all the days of my life, and I will dwell in the house of the LORD forever.

PSALM 23:1–6 NIV

Oh, that you would burst from the heavens and come down!
How the mountains would quake in your presence! As fire
causes wood to burn and water to boil, your coming would
make the nations tremble. Then your enemies would learn
the reason for your fame! When you came down long ago,
you did awesome deeds beyond our highest expectations.
And oh, how the mountains quaked! For since the world
began, no ear has heard and no eye has seen a God like you,
who works for those who wait for him!

ISAIAH 64:1–4 NLT

"My soul glorifies the Lord and my spirit rejoices in God my
Savior, for he has been mindful of the humble state of his
servant. From now on all generations will call me blessed,
for the Mighty One has done great things for me—holy is
his name. His mercy extends to those who fear him, from
generation to generation. He has performed mighty deeds with
his arm; he has scattered those who are proud in their inmost
thoughts. He has brought down rulers from their thrones but
has lifted up the humble. He has filled the hungry with good
things but has sent the rich away empty. He has helped his
servant Israel, remembering to be merciful to Abraham and his
descendants forever, just as he promised our ancestors."

LUKE 1:46–55 NIV

For this reason, ever since I heard about your faith in the Lord Jesus and your love for all God's people, I have not stopped giving thanks for you, remembering you in my prayers. I keep asking that the God of our Lord Jesus Christ, the glorious Father, may give you the Spirit of wisdom and revelation, so that you may know him better. I pray that the eyes of your heart may be enlightened in order that you may know the hope to which he has called you, the riches of his glorious inheritance in his holy people, and his incomparably great power for us who believe. That power is the same as the mighty strength he exerted when he raised Christ from the dead and seated him at his right hand in the heavenly realms, far above all rule and authority, power and dominion, and every name that is invoked, not only in the present age but also in the one to come. And God placed all things under his feet and appointed him to be head over everything for the church, which is his body, the fullness of him who fills everything in every way.

EPHESIANS 1:15–23 NIV

"O Sovereign LORD! You made the heavens and earth by your strong hand and powerful arm. Nothing is too hard for you! You show unfailing love to thousands, but you also bring the consequences of one generation's sin upon the next. You are the great and powerful God, the LORD of Heaven's Armies. You have all wisdom and do great and mighty miracles. You see the conduct of all people, and you give them what they deserve. You performed miraculous signs and wonders in the land of Egypt—things still remembered to this day! And you have continued to do great miracles in Israel and all around the world. You have made your name famous to this day."

JEREMIAH 32:17–20 NLT

Oh, the depth of the riches of the wisdom and knowledge of God! How unsearchable his judgments, and his paths beyond tracing out! "Who has known the mind of the Lord? Or who has been his counselor?" "Who has ever given to God, that God should repay them?" For from him and through him and for him are all things. To him be the glory forever! Amen.

ROMANS 11:33–36 NIV

Everyday Promises

God's Word is full of answers, promises, and loving guidance. The best news of all is that we are offered words of hope, an outstretched hand of comfort, and the promise of God's unchanging, unfailing Word.

Connect with the One who stands behind each and every promise. Each of these scripture selections will bless your heart and soothe your spirit. Hallelujah!

"*You have done this great thing and made known all these great promises.*"

1 Chronicles 17:19 niv

But you are a tower of refuge to the poor, O LORD, a tower of refuge to the needy in distress. You are a refuge from the storm and a shelter from the heat. For the oppressive acts of ruthless people are like a storm beating against a wall, or like the relentless heat of the desert. But you silence the roar of foreign nations. As the shade of a cloud cools relentless heat, so the boastful songs of ruthless people are stilled.

ISAIAH 25:4–5 NLT

We are pressed on every side by troubles, but we are not crushed. We are perplexed, but not driven to despair. We are hunted down, but never abandoned by God. We get knocked down, but we are not destroyed. Through suffering, our bodies continue to share in the death of Jesus so that the life of Jesus may also be seen in our bodies.

2 CORINTHIANS 4:8–10 NLT

And we know that God causes all things to work
together for good to those who love God,
to those who are called according to His purpose.

ROMANS 8:28 NASB

But, as it is written, "What no eye has seen, nor ear heard,
nor the heart of man imagined, what God has prepared for
those who love him"—these things God has revealed to us
through the Spirit. For the Spirit searches
everything, even the depths of God.

1 CORINTHIANS 2:9–10 ESV

Then Christ will make his home in your hearts as you trust in
him. Your roots will grow down into God's love and keep you
strong. And may you have the power to understand, as all God's
people should, how wide, how long, how high, and how deep
his love is. May you experience the love of Christ, though it is
too great to understand fully. Then you will be made complete
with all the fullness of life and power that comes from God.

EPHESIANS 3:17–19 NLT

"But the Advocate, the Holy Spirit, whom the Father
will send in my name, will teach you all things and
will remind you of everything I have said to you."
JOHN 14:26 NIV

Peter replied, "Repent and be baptized, every one of you,
in the name of Jesus Christ for the forgiveness of your sins.
And you will receive the gift of the Holy Spirit. The promise
is for you and your children and for all who are far off—
for all whom the Lord our God will call."
ACTS 2:38–39 NIV

But do not forget this one thing, dear friends: With the Lord
a day is like a thousand years, and a thousand years are like
a day. The Lord is not slow in keeping his promise, as some
understand slowness. Instead he is patient with you, not
wanting anyone to perish, but everyone to come to repentance.
But the day of the Lord will come like a thief. The heavens will
disappear with a roar; the elements will be destroyed by fire,
and the earth and everything done in it will be laid bare.
2 PETER 3:8–10 NIV

"To me this is like the days of Noah, when I swore that the waters of Noah would never again cover the earth. So now I have sworn not to be angry with you, never to rebuke you again. Though the mountains be shaken and the hills be removed, yet my unfailing love for you will not be shaken nor my covenant of peace be removed," says the LORD, who has compassion on you.

ISAIAH 54:9–10 NIV

Give thanks to the Lord, for he is good! His faithful love endures forever. Cry out, "Save us, O God of our salvation! Gather and rescue us from among the nations, so we can thank your holy name and rejoice and praise you." Praise the Lord, the God of Israel, who lives from everlasting to everlasting! And all the people shouted "Amen!" and praised the Lord.

1 CHRONICLES 16:34–36 NLT

They will come home and sing songs of joy on the heights of Jerusalem. They will be radiant because of the LORD's good gifts—the abundant crops of grain, new wine, and olive oil, and the healthy flocks and herds. Their life will be like a watered garden, and all their sorrows will be gone.

JEREMIAH 31:12 NLT

Some people make cutting remarks, but the words of the wise bring healing. Truthful words stand the test of time, but lies are soon exposed. Deceit fills hearts that are plotting evil; joy fills hearts that are planning peace! No harm comes to the godly, but the wicked have their fill of trouble. The LORD detests lying lips, but he delights in those who tell the truth.

PROVERBS 12:18–22 NLT

The fear of the LORD prolongs life, but the years of the wicked will be shortened. The hope of the righteous is gladness, but the expectation of the wicked perishes. The way of the LORD is a stronghold to the upright, but ruin to the workers of iniquity. The righteous will never be shaken, but the wicked will not dwell in the land. The mouth of the righteous flows with wisdom, but the perverted tongue will be cut out. The lips of the righteous bring forth what is acceptable, but the mouth of the wicked what is perverted.

PROVERBS 10:27–32 NASB

Command those who are rich in this present world not
to be arrogant nor to put their hope in wealth, which is so
uncertain, but to put their hope in God, who richly provides
us with everything for our enjoyment. Command them to do
good, to be rich in good deeds, and to be generous and willing
to share. In this way they will lay up treasure for themselves
as a firm foundation for the coming age, so that they
may take hold of the life that is truly life.
1 TIMOTHY 6:17–19 NIV

"So do not worry, saying, 'What shall we eat?' or 'What shall
we drink?' or 'What shall we wear?' For the pagans run after
all these things, and your heavenly Father knows that you
need them. But seek first his kingdom and his righteousness,
and all these things will be given to you as well."
MATTHEW 6:31–33 NIV

And my God will meet all your needs according
to the riches of his glory in Christ Jesus.
PHILIPPIANS 4:19 NIV

He who pursues righteousness and loyalty
finds life, righteousness and honor.
PROVERBS 21:21 NASB

To humans belong the plans of the heart, but from the
LORD comes the proper answer of the tongue. All a person's
ways seem pure to them, but motives are weighed by the
LORD. Commit to the LORD whatever you do, and he will
establish your plans. The LORD works out everything to its
proper end—even the wicked for a day of disaster. The LORD
detests all the proud of heart. Be sure of this: They will not go
unpunished. Through love and faithfulness sin is atoned for;
through the fear of the LORD evil is avoided. When the
LORD takes pleasure in anyone's way, he causes their
enemies to make peace with them.
PROVERBS 16:1–7 NIV

For physical training is of some value, but godliness
has value for all things, holding promise for both
the present life and the life to come. This is a
trustworthy saying that deserves full acceptance.
1 TIMOTHY 4:8–9 NIV

The wise woman builds her house, but the foolish tears it down with her own hands. He who walks in his uprightness fears the LORD, but he who is devious in his ways despises Him. In the mouth of the foolish is a rod for his back, but the lips of the wise will protect them.

PROVERBS 14:1–3 NASB

A joyful heart makes a cheerful face, but when the heart is sad, the spirit is broken. The mind of the intelligent seeks knowledge, but the mouth of fools feeds on folly. All the days of the afflicted are bad, but a cheerful heart has a continual feast. Better is a little with the fear of the LORD than great treasure and turmoil with it.

PROVERBS 15:13–16 NASB

For the word of the LORD is right and true; he is faithful in all he does. The LORD loves righteousness and justice; the earth is full of his unfailing love.

PSALM 33:4–5 NIV

But the LORD watches over those who fear him, those who rely on his unfailing love. He rescues them from death and keeps them alive in times of famine. We put our hope in the LORD. He is our help and our shield. In him our hearts rejoice, for we trust in his holy name. Let your unfailing love surround us, LORD, for our hope is in you alone.

PSALM 33:18–22 NLT

"If my people who are called by my name humble themselves, and pray and seek my face and turn from their wicked ways, then I will hear from heaven and will forgive their sin and heal their land. Now my eyes will be open and my ears attentive to the prayer that is made in this place."

2 CHRONICLES 7:14–15 ESV

The integrity of the upright will guide them, but the crookedness of the treacherous will destroy them. Riches do not profit in the day of wrath, but righteousness delivers from death. The righteousness of the blameless will smooth his way, but the wicked will fall by his own wickedness. The righteousness of the upright will deliver them, but the treacherous will be caught by their own greed. When a wicked man dies, his expectation will perish, and the hope of strong men perishes. The righteous is delivered from trouble, but the wicked takes his place.

PROVERBS 11:3–8 NASB

Surely your goodness and love will follow me all the days of my life, and I will dwell in the house of the LORD forever.

PSALM 23:6 NIV

For the LORD God is a sun and shield; the LORD bestows favor and honor; no good thing does he withhold from those whose walk is blameless. LORD Almighty, blessed is the one who trusts in you.

PSALM 84:11–12 NIV

Everyday Thanks

We worship a living God, the Creator of all things. Though just and holy, our God is also loving and tenderhearted. He breathes and speaks and hears. Of all the people on earth, those who worship the name of the Lord should be thankful, for He is alive! He cares when we are hurting; He has the power and the willingness to help us in our time of need.

Your heart will swell with thankfulness and joy as you read the following Bible promises, for our God is a great God. He is good and generous and kind. Give thanks!

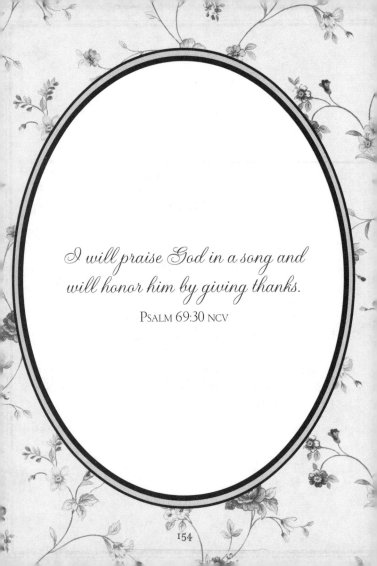

*I will praise God in a song and
will honor him by giving thanks.*

Psalm 69:30 NCV

I give you thanks, O LORD, with all my heart; I will sing
your praises before the gods. I bow before your holy Temple
as I worship. I praise your name for your unfailing love and
faithfulness; for your promises are backed by all the honor
of your name. As soon as I pray, you answer me;
you encourage me by giving me strength.
PSALM 138:1–3 NLT

You turned my wailing into dancing; you removed
my sackcloth and clothed me with joy, that my heart
may sing your praises and not be silent.
LORD my God, I will praise you forever.
PSALM 30:11–12 NIV

"The time is coming when the true worshipers will
worship the Father in spirit and truth, and that time is
here already. You see, the Father too is actively seeking
such people to worship him. God is spirit, and those
who worship him must worship in spirit and truth."
JOHN 4:23–24 NCV

And so, dear brothers and sisters, I plead with you to give
your bodies to God because of all he has done for you.
Let them be a living and holy sacrifice—the kind he will
find acceptable. This is truly the way to worship him.
Don't copy the behavior and customs of this world, but let
God transform you into a new person by changing the way
you think. Then you will learn to know God's will
for you, which is good and pleasing and perfect.
ROMANS 12:1–2 NLT

Thanks be to God for his gift that is too wonderful for words.
2 CORINTHIANS 9:15 NCV

But thanks be to God, who always leads us as captives in
Christ's victory parade. God uses us to spread his knowledge
everywhere like a sweet-smelling perfume. Our offering to
God is this: We are the sweet smell of Christ among those
who are being saved and among those who are being lost.
2 CORINTHIANS 2:14–15 NCV

The sting of death is sin, and the power of sin
is the law. But thanks be to God! He gives
us the victory through our Lord Jesus Christ.
1 CORINTHIANS 15:56–57 NIV

We know that God, who raised the Lord Jesus, will also
raise us with Jesus and present us to himself together
with you. All of this is for your benefit. And as God's
grace reaches more and more people, there will be great
thanksgiving, and God will receive more and more glory.
That is why we never give up. Though our bodies are
dying, our spirits are being renewed every day.
2 CORINTHIANS 4:14–16 NLT

Do not be anxious about anything,
but in every situation, by prayer and petition,
with thanksgiving, present your requests to God.
PHILIPPIANS 4:6 NIV

Speak to each other with psalms, hymns, and spiritual songs,
singing and making music in your hearts to the Lord.
Always give thanks to God the Father for everything,
in the name of our Lord Jesus Christ.
EPHESIANS 5:19–20 NCV

Therefore, as you received Christ Jesus the Lord, so walk in
him, rooted and built up in him and established in the faith,
just as you were taught, abounding in thanksgiving.
COLOSSIANS 2:6–7 ESV

Let the teaching of Christ live in you richly. Use all
wisdom to teach and instruct each other by singing
psalms, hymns, and spiritual songs with thankfulness in
your hearts to God. Everything you do or say should
be done to obey Jesus your Lord. And in all you do,
give thanks to God the Father through Jesus.
COLOSSIANS 3:16–17 NCV

Rejoice always, pray continually, give thanks in all
circumstances; for this is God's will for you in Christ Jesus.
1 THESSALONIANS 5:16–18 NIV

Since everything God created is good,
we should not reject any of it but receive it with thanks.
1 TIMOTHY 4:4 NLT

And they said, "We give thanks to you, Lord God, the
Almighty, the one who is and who always was, for now you
have assumed your great power and have begun to reign."
REVELATION 11:17 NLT

You will say in that day: "I will give thanks to you, O LORD,
for though you were angry with me, your anger turned away,
that you might comfort me. Behold, God is my salvation; I
will trust, and will not be afraid; for the LORD GOD is my
strength and my song, and he has become my salvation."
With joy you will draw water from the wells of salvation.
ISAIAH 12:1–3 ESV

I will give to the LORD the thanks due to his
righteousness, and I will sing praise to the
name of the LORD, the Most High.
PSALM 7:17 ESV

Give your burdens to the Lord, and he will take care
of you. He will not permit the godly to slip and fall.
PSALM 55:22 NLT

The LORD is my strength and shield. I trust him with
all my heart. He helps me, and my heart is filled with joy.
I burst out in songs of thanksgiving.
PSALM 28:7 NLT

In God we have boasted continually,
and we will give thanks to your name forever.
PSALM 44:8 ESV

Teach me your way, O LORD, that I may walk in your truth;
unite my heart to fear your name. I give thanks to you,
O Lord my God, with my whole heart, and I will glorify your
name forever. For great is your steadfast love toward me; you
have delivered my soul from the depths of Sheol.

PSALM 86:11–13 ESV

Come, let's sing for joy to the LORD. Let's shout praises to
the Rock who saves us. Let's come to him with thanksgiving.
Let's sing songs to him, because the LORD is the
great God, the great King over all gods.

PSALM 95:1–3 NCV

Give thanks to the LORD, for he is good; his love endures
forever. Let the redeemed of the LORD tell their story—those
he redeemed from the hand of the foe, those he gathered from
the lands, from east and west, from north and south.

PSALM 107:1–3 NIV

I will fulfill my vows to you, O God,
and will offer a sacrifice of thanks for your help.

PSALM 56:12 NLT

Let them give thanks to the LORD for his unfailing love
and his wonderful deeds for mankind, for he satisfies
the thirsty and fills the hungry with good things.
PSALM 107:8–9 NIV

I will give you an offering to show thanks to you, and I will
pray to the LORD. I will give the LORD what I promised in
front of all his people, in the Temple courtyards in Jerusalem.
Praise the LORD!
PSALM 116:17–19 NCV

Therefore, since we are receiving a kingdom that
cannot be shaken, let us give thanks, by which we
offer to God an acceptable worship with reverence
and awe; for indeed our God is a consuming fire.
HEBREWS 12:28–29 NRSV

The LORD is God, and he has made his light to shine
upon us. Bind the festal sacrifice with cords, up to the horns
of the altar! You are my God, and I will give thanks to you;
you are my God; I will extol you. Oh give thanks to the LORD,
for he is good; for his steadfast love endures forever!
PSALM 118:27–29 ESV

"So do not fear, for I am with you;
do not be dismayed, for I am your God.
I will strengthen you and help you; I will
uphold you with my righteous right hand."
ISAIAH 41:10 NIV

Skies, sing for joy because the LORD did great things!
Earth, shout for joy, even in your deepest parts! Sing, you
mountains, with thanks to God. Sing, too, you trees in the
forest! The LORD saved the people of Jacob! He showed his
glory when he saved Israel. This is what the LORD says,
who saved you, who formed you in your mother's body:
"I, the LORD, made everything, stretching out the skies
by myself and spreading out the earth all alone.

ISAIAH 44:23–24 NCV

"There will be heard once more the sounds of joy and
gladness, the voices of bride and bridegroom, and the voices
of those who bring thank offerings to the house of the LORD,
saying, 'Give thanks to the LORD Almighty, for the LORD is
good; his love endures forever.' For I will restore the fortunes
of the land as they were before,' says the LORD."

JEREMIAH 33:10–11 NIV

Everyday Wisdom

Regardless of your age, position, or season, you're invited to walk with and learn from the source of all wisdom, God Himself. He knows you better than you know yourself, and He cares—about your secret dreams, financial struggles, career woes, and family dynamics.

The Bible promises on the pages that follow will help you develop a richer relationship with our awesome God and give you a deeper glimpse of His knowledge. As you allow God's Word to sink deep into your heart, you'll grow to recognize your options, make wise choices, and take intentional action—which is just what the heavenly Father wants for you!

How much better to get wisdom than gold, and good judgment than silver!

PROVERBS 16:16 NLT

To know wisdom and instruction, to understand words of insight, to receive instruction in wise dealing, in righteousness, justice, and equity; to give prudence to the simple, knowledge and discretion to the youth—let the wise hear and increase in learning, and the one who understands obtain guidance. . . .
The fear of the Lord is the beginning of knowledge; fools despise wisdom and instruction.

Proverbs 1:2–5, 7 esv

If you receive my words and treasure up my commandments with you, making your ear attentive to wisdom and inclining your heart to understanding; yes, if you call out for insight and raise your voice for understanding, if you seek it like silver and search for it as for hidden treasures, then you will understand the fear of the Lord and find the knowledge of God. For the Lord gives wisdom; from his mouth come knowledge and understanding.

Proverbs 2:1–6 esv

The instructions of the LORD are perfect, reviving the soul. The decrees of the LORD are trustworthy, making wise the simple. The commandments of the LORD are right, bringing joy to the heart. The commands of the LORD are clear, giving insight for living.

PSALM 19:7–8 NLT

O nations of the world, recognize the LORD; recognize that the LORD is glorious and strong. Give to the LORD the glory he deserves! Bring your offering and come into his courts. Worship the LORD in all his holy splendor. Let all the earth tremble before him.

PSALM 96:7–9 NLT

Like clouds and wind without rain is a man who boasts of a gift he does not give.

PROVERBS 25:14 ESV

In the house of the righteous there is much treasure, but trouble befalls the income of the wicked.

PROVERBS 15:6 ESV

Your word is a lamp for my feet, a light on my path. . . .
The unfolding of your words gives light;
it gives understanding to the simple.
PSALM 119:105, 130 NIV

But as for me, it is good to be near God. I have made the
Sovereign LORD my refuge; I will tell of all your deeds.
PSALM 73:28 NIV

Unless the LORD builds a house, the work of the
builders is wasted. Unless the LORD protects a city,
guarding it with sentries will do no good.
PSALM 127:1 NLT

Work with enthusiasm, as though you were
working for the Lord rather than for people.
EPHESIANS 6:7 NLT

The Lord is my shepherd, I lack nothing. He makes
me lie down in green pastures, he leads me beside
quiet waters, he refreshes my soul. He guides me
along the right paths for his name's sake.
PSALM 23:1–3 NIV

If you plan to do evil, you will be lost; if you plan to do good,
you will receive unfailing love and faithfulness. Work brings
profit, but mere talk leads to poverty! Wealth is a crown for
the wise; the effort of fools yields only foolishness.
PROVERBS 14:22–24 NLT

Good planning and hard work lead to prosperity,
but hasty shortcuts lead to poverty. Wealth created
by a lying tongue is a vanishing mist and a deadly trap.
PROVERBS 21:5–6 NLT

A hard worker has plenty of food, but a person who chases fantasies has no sense. . . . Work hard and become a leader; be lazy and become a slave. . . . Lazy people don't even cook the game they catch, but the diligent make use of everything they find.
PROVERBS 12:11, 24, 27 NLT

A sluggard's appetite is never filled, but the desires of the diligent are fully satisfied.
PROVERBS 13:4 NIV

The greedy stir up conflict, but those who trust in the LORD will prosper.
PROVERBS 28:25 NIV

Then he said to them, "Watch out! Be on your guard against all kinds of greed; life does not consist in an abundance of possessions."
LUKE 12:15 NIV

For of this you can be sure: No immoral, impure or greedy person—such a person is an idolater—has any inheritance in the kingdom of Christ and of God.

EPHESIANS 5:5 NIV

She gets up while it is still night; she provides food for her family and portions for her female servants. She considers a field and buys it; out of her earnings she plants a vineyard. She sets about her work vigorously; her arms are strong for her tasks. She sees that her trading is profitable, and her lamp does not go out at night. . . . She opens her arms to the poor and extends her hands to the needy. When it snows, she has no fear for her household; for all of them are clothed in scarlet.

PROVERBS 31:15–18, 20–21 NIV

The mouths of fools are their undoing, and their lips are a snare to their very lives. The words of a gossip are like choice morsels; they go down to the inmost parts.

PROVERBS 18:7–8 NIV

"Do not store up for yourselves treasures on earth,
where moths and vermin destroy, and where thieves
break in and steal. But store up for yourselves treasures
in heaven, where moths and vermin do not destroy,
and where thieves do not break in and steal. For where
your treasure is, there your heart will be also."
MATTHEW 6:19–21 NIV

This is the message we heard from Jesus and now declare
to you: God is light, and there is no darkness in him at all.
So we are lying if we say we have fellowship with God but go
on living in spiritual darkness; we are not practicing the truth.
But if we are living in the light, as God is in the light,
then we have fellowship with each other, and the blood
of Jesus, his Son, cleanses us from all sin.
1 JOHN 1:5–7 NLT

"Abide in Me, and I in you. As the branch cannot
bear fruit of itself, unless it abides in the vine, neither
can you, unless you abide in Me. I am the vine, you
are the branches. He who abides in Me, and I in him,
bears much fruit; for without Me you can do nothing."
JOHN 15:4–5 NKJV

One who has unreliable friends soon comes to ruin,
but there is a friend who sticks closer than a brother.
PROVERBS 18:24 NIV

They are to do good, to be rich in good works, to be
generous and ready to share, thus storing up treasure
for themselves as a good foundation for the future,
so that they may take hold of that which is truly life.
1 TIMOTHY 6:18–19 ESV

One of the teachers of religious law was standing there listening to the debate. He realized that Jesus had answered well, so he asked, "Of all the commandments, which is the most important?" Jesus replied, "The most important commandment is this: 'Listen, O Israel! The LORD our God is the one and only LORD. And you must love the LORD your God with all your heart, all your soul, all your mind, and all your strength.' The second is equally important: 'Love your neighbor as yourself.' No other commandment is greater than these."

MARK 12:28–31 NLT

Don't let anyone capture you with empty philosophies and high-sounding nonsense that come from human thinking and from the spiritual powers of this world, rather than from Christ. For in Christ lives all the fullness of God in a human body. So you also are complete through your union with Christ, who is the head over every ruler and authority.

COLOSSIANS 2:8–10 NLT

Don't copy the behavior and customs of this world,
but let God transform you into a new person by changing
the way you think. Then you will learn to know God's
will for you, which is good and pleasing and perfect.
ROMANS 12:2 NLT

By wisdom a house is built, and through understanding
it is established; through knowledge its rooms
are filled with rare and beautiful treasures.
PROVERBS 24:3–4 NIV

Now may the God of peace, who through the blood of
the eternal covenant brought back from the dead our
Lord Jesus, that great Shepherd of the sheep, equip you
with everything good for doing his will, and may he
work in us what is pleasing to him, through Jesus Christ,
to whom be glory for ever and ever. Amen.
HEBREWS 13:20–21 NIV